A Promise at Sobibór

A Promise at Sobibór

*A Jewish Boy's Story of Revolt and
Survival in Nazi-Occupied Poland*

Philip "Fiszel" Bialowitz,

with

Joseph Bialowitz

The University of Wisconsin Press

Publication of this book has been aided by a gift in memory of
Laurence A. Weinstein.

The University of Wisconsin Press
1930 Monroe Street, 3rd Floor
Madison, Wisconsin 53711-2059
uwpress.wisc.edu

3 Henrietta Street
London WCE 8LU, England
eurospanbookstore.com

An earlier version of this book was published in Polish as *Bunt w Sobiborze* by Philip Bialowitz and
Joseph Bialowitz, copyright © 2008 by Philip Bialowitz.

5   4   3   2   1

Printed in the United States of America

Library of Congress Cataloging-in-Publication Data
Bialowitz, Philip, 1925–
[Bunt w Sobiborze. English]
A promise at Sobibór: a Jewish boy's story of revolt and survival in Nazi-occupied Poland /
    Philip "Fiszel" Bialowitz, with Joseph Bialowitz.
       p.   cm.
       Includes bibliographical references.
       ISBN 978-0-299-24800-0 (cloth: alk. paper)
       ISBN 978-0-299-24803-1 (e-book)
1. Bialowitz, Philip, 1925–   2. Jews—Poland—Izbica Lubelska—Biography.
    3. Holocaust, Jewish (1939–1945)—Poland—Personal narratives.   4. Sobibór
    (Concentration camp)   5. Concentration camp escapes—Poland—Sobibór.
    6. Concentration camp inmates—Poland—Sobibór—Biography.   7. World
    War, 1939–1945—Jewish resistance.   I. Bialowitz, Joseph, 1974–   II. Title.
DS134.72.B527A3   2010
940.53′18092—dc22
[B]
2010014290

Frontispiece (page ii): Philip Bialowitz as a partisan in 1943, several days after escaping from Sobibór.
Photo in author's private collection.

To the millions who perished and whose stories will never be told

To the righteous people who tried to save others

To my daughter Evelyn, who gave me courage and strength

Happiness is always where a person sees it.
Henryk Sienkiewicz, *Quo Vadis*

Contents

Foreword

The memory of the Holocaust is, above all, the memory of murdered people. The terrible abyss of evil that destroyed millions of lives during the last world war provokes a sense of shock and disbelief that cannot be expressed in words. We must consider how such atrocities could have been possible. It is a most difficult task for Jews because they are still mourning—and will indeed always mourn—their millions of murdered relatives.

The fate of Jews in German-occupied Europe was decided in January 1942 at the Wannsee Conference in Berlin, where the Third Reich made its decision regarding "the final solution to the Jewish question." However, the Germans disguised their intentions to murder all of Europe's Jewish inhabitants. In the history of civilization, there has never been such a methodical plan of mass killing and looting, bringing to bear the enormous forces of human and industrial procedures in an effort to murder. Hitler's propaganda first deprived Jews of their humanity, equating them with vermin. These Jews were then isolated and terrorized in the centers of mass destruction, murdered in ways that beggar description. As a result, German Nazism led to an outcome that few could have even imagined: the destruction of Jewish civilization throughout a significant part of Europe.

In view of this inconceivable tragedy, we should remember with all the more admiration those Jews who successfully fought against their

Translated from the Polish original and used by permission of Władysław Bartoszewski and Wydawnictwo Nasza Księgarnia.

tormentors, the Germans and their collaborators. Each Jew was, from the perspective of the German occupiers, a being who deserved to be destroyed. A Jew who encountered a German soldier or policeman met not only his mortal enemy in war but also someone who believed that Jews did not have the right to life. But how can people maintain their will to live when they sense that their deaths are imminent? When we speak of the Jewish resistance movement in the death camps, we should keep in mind that these camps, by definition, prevented any opportunity to confront the Germans. Revolts that occurred in the camps in Treblinka, Sobibór, and Auschwitz-Birkenau are further proof that Jews showed their murderers that one cannot destroy their humanity. The fact that a few prisoners managed to survive was extremely important. It meant that the Holocaust would be a crime that could not be forgotten.

Philip "Fiszel" Bialowitz, a former prisoner at the Sobibór extermination camp, has written of his personal history of struggle. He has described how a group of several hundred Jews decided to avenge the deaths of their relatives, friends, and other victims, and of how Sobibór was the scene of an unprecedented event: a dramatic escape of prisoners en masse. He wrote this book out of his wish to fulfill the mission entrusted to him at Sobibór on October 14, 1943. There, seconds before the prisoner uprising began, the revolt leaders—a rabbi's son from Żółkiewka named Leon Feldhendler and a Soviet Army soldier named Sasha Pechersky—called out to their fellow prisoners: "If you survive, bear witness to what happened here! Tell the world about this place!"

For many years, Philip Bialowitz has been testifying about what he witnessed to the many of us who wish to learn. He speaks at synagogues, churches, universities, schools, and museums around the world. His message is not only a shocking description of the fate of humankind or a cry of despair for the millions of innocent victims but also—and above all—a clarion call that never again in human history can we allow hatred and indifference to create such tragedy. Philip Bialowitz is an extremely strong voice of humanity's conscience. He recognizes that today's world contains new "Holocausts," and he points to them and condemns them. More than six decades after the revolt at Sobibór, readers now have in their hands a very significant book that is a unique testimony of truth about history's darkest moment.

WŁADYSŁAW BARTOSZEWSKI

Secretary of State, Republic of Poland
Plenipotentiary of the Council of Ministers on International Dialogue and Affairs
Member of the Righteous among the Nations
Honorary Citizen of the State of Israel

Preface

I wrote this book with the humble hope that it will enable readers to imagine themselves in the situations that I faced as a teenager. This required using my boyhood voice to relive my teenage years in "real time." Through hundreds of hours of interviews, I worked with my son Joseph to recount my experiences and record them without the benefit of hindsight. If I seemed to be coloring a story with a perspective that I might have gained after the event itself, Joseph reminded me to limit myself to recalling only what I knew "back then." If my after-the-fact knowledge helped to explain the context of an event, we agreed to communicate these historical details in notes.

My depiction of each event included in this book is completely factual according to the best of my memory. Although I have made every effort to recount the events in the order that they actually occurred, some inaccuracies in chronology may nevertheless remain. Similarly, my ability to remember the names of people involved in these long-ago events is limited; I therefore apologize for possible errors associated with any of the names listed throughout the book. Furthermore, total recall of dialogues was not always possible more than sixty years after they occurred, and I therefore took the liberty of reconstructing some dialogues. Specifically, I reconstructed—to the best of my recollection—the informal conversations that took place between me and my family members and friends. And while verbatim reconstruction is, of course, largely impossible after six decades have passed, many of the book's other dialogues—including those involving schoolchildren, SS personnel, resistance fighters inside and outside Sobibór, civilian rescuers, Soviet soldiers, and Soviet secret police—were so forceful and significant that I remember them quite clearly and believe that, to a great degree, I have faithfully recorded them according to their tone and actual content.

The Polish historian Robert Kuwalek provided several historical elaborations, based primarily on Polish-language sources, within the notes of my Polish-language memoir, *Bunt w Sobiborze*. These informative elaborations form the basis of several notes within this English-language edition. Readers wishing to consult Mr. Kuwalek's sources should refer to the respective pages in *Bunt w Sobiborze* that I have listed in all notes citing *Bunt w Sobiborze* as their source.

Finally, I am grateful to many selfless individuals who helped to produce this book. Joseph devoted himself to this project with characteristic patience and determination. My brother Symcha, without whose love and protection I would not be alive today, helped me to describe our shared experiences in more vivid detail, especially the circumstances of his plot to poison the SS members who worked at Sobibór. My close friends Henry Kleinman and Samuel Peltz lived through several of the same events that I experienced in Izbica, and their sharp memories helped me to better recall the circumstances of these events. My editors, Hanh Bui, Daniel Housman, and Barb Wojhoski, provided generous, meticulous, and thoughtful input, helping me to maintain a consistent voice throughout the book. Michael Green was one of the first to recognize the power of my story and contributed the basic format that I used to structure my narrative. The heartfelt foreword written by Władysław Bartoszewski for *Bunt w Sobiborze* (and reprinted here) represents just one of many gifts that this great man has contributed to the world; I hope that readers will seek to learn more about Professor Bartoszewski and his lifetime of inspirational work. Anna Witkowska provided meaningful insights into Polish history while assisting with Polish translations and spelling conventions. Anna Garbal of the Nasza Księgarnia publishing house was kind enough to authorize the reprinting of illustrations originally contained in my Polish-language memoir. Raphael Kadushin, Katie Malchow, and Sheila Moermond of the University of Wisconsin Press skillfully assisted with preparing this book for publication. Michele Cooper, Meghan Adler, and Robin Nagel provided valuable comments on early manuscript versions. Uwe Kaminski and Anne Bernhardt located German archival information about the Rosenberger family and assisted with German translations. Ben Mirus researched the fate of Gustav Wagner and provided translation assistance with German-language sources. Manuel Aalbers and Janneke Roukema worked with me to identify the Dutch melody that I learned at Sobibór. Vera Kartseva lent guidance on Russian naming conventions. Professor Shevach Weiss, former United States Ambassador Victor Ashe, Aleksandra Skibniewska, Albert Stankowski, and Poland's chief rabbi, Michael Schudrich, each encouraged me to share my message with the people of Poland and the rest of the world.

Introduction

Between the ages of thirteen and eighteen, my father was targeted for murder along with everyone he loved. Nearly all of them perished. Yet somehow my father was able to survive.

I was thirteen years old when I first learned that my father was a survivor of a Nazi death camp named Sobibór, where an estimated 250,000 Jews were murdered in near-daily executions between 1942 and 1943. But I also discovered that Sobibór was the scene of the largest and most successful prisoner revolt of World War II, in which a small group of conspirators managed to free about 200 of the camp's 650 Jewish slave laborers.

Like a typical teenager, I yearned to know as much as possible about my father's own boyhood years. I began asking questions, and—no matter how difficult it was—my father was willing to provide answers. His memories were still fresh and detailed:

"There was a Jewish Gestapo officer."

"I was covered in other people's blood."

"Even my seven-year-old niece knew she was going to die."

"Her skin remained in my hands."

"I was only a teenager. I wanted to live."

"We killed the Nazis one by one."

I listened to my father's emotional accounts of his past with greater and greater interest because, in addition to teaching me about his life, they helped to explain the differences I was beginning to sense between my family and the families of my friends. Why did my siblings and I attend synagogue when we would rather be playing soccer? Why did all my friends have four grandparents while I had two? The answers I gathered only led to more questions. Who were these grandparents, aunts, uncles, and cousins whom I had never met? Why did they—and millions of other people—die at the hands of murderers? How in the world did my father live to tell about it? And what could prevent similar tragedies from happening again?

Much about the Holocaust will always remain inexplicable. Indeed, why nine out of ten European Jewish children alive in 1939 had to die is one question that nobody will ever be able to fully answer. But if there could be a single explanation for how so many were murdered, it is that millions of people must have made decisions—some abominable, some mundane—in the daily moments of their lives that helped to perpetuate evil. Similarly, we know that of the "lucky" few who survived the Holocaust, many did so because someone risked something—sometimes his or her life, sometimes comparatively little—in order to help. Concerning the fundamental choices that people faced, Elie Wiesel has remarked, "Remember that it was easy to save human lives. One did not need to be heroic or crazy to feel pity for an abandoned child. It was enough to open a door, to throw a piece of bread, a shirt, a coin—it was enough to feel compassion. . . . In those times, one climbed to the summit of humanity by simply remaining human."[1] But if retaining one's humanity required so little, why did so many people act like beasts? And how were people able to remain human even while clawing to survive? Perhaps the only way to attempt to answer these questions is by deeply examining the lives led by people like my father and those around him before, during, and after the Holocaust.

In order to develop a semblance of appreciation for these individual stories, in 1999 I accompanied my father on my first trip to Poland. I could never truly know what it was like for them, but at least I could visit the towns in which my relatives lived and the places in which they perished more than thirty years before I was born. I spent several days in Izbica, where much of my family had lived for generations, eating fruit and vegetables from the same soil that they had eaten from, exploring the same dirt roads and forests where they had once walked, offering Jewish prayers in the cemetery where they had once mourned, and feeling what the weather felt like during a certain time of the year. After gaining this sensory connection with their lives, I was then ready to join my father in visiting some of the Nazi camps where they had been murdered: Sobibór, Auschwitz, Majdanek, and Treblinka. These monuments to evil were not easy to confront, but my experience of these places brought me closer to my relatives by once again providing me with a tiny, physical experience of what they had likely gone through. For example, at Sobibór and Treblinka I had planned to spend some quiet moments reflecting and perhaps offering a prayer. Only when I arrived did I realize that my plan was impossible to carry out. The Nazis had hid both of these camps in the deep forest, and during the early summer months I was getting eaten alive by mosquitoes and bees whenever I stood still. If it was this bad for me, I thought, then how much more wretched must it have been for prisoners like my father and those who were forced to their deaths naked in these places?

Although so many of them ultimately died at the hands of the Nazi Germans, people like my father honored life and human dignity by never abandoning hope and by engaging in myriad forms of resistance. The persistent myth that Jews went to their deaths "like sheep to the slaughter" is dispelled by the heroic uprisings of Jews at Sobibór and many other places, most notably the Warsaw Ghetto. Resistance groups were active in approximately one hundred Eastern European ghettos, up to twenty thousand Jews fought as partisans in the forests of Eastern Europe, and at least one million Jews served in the Allied armies. Although it is true that many other Jews did not engage in armed resistance, they often fought for their lives in important ways: they went into hiding; they obtained false identity papers; they fled to other countries; they even sent their children to be raised by strangers abroad. They also derived the strength to go on living by praying and observing what religious traditions they could and continuing to school their children.

But from what wellspring did my father derive his strength? Interviewing my father for this book revealed to me that his indomitable spirit and passion for life were qualities that he possessed long before they were tested by the Nazis. His instinct for survival during the Holocaust was not rooted in fear; rather, it was made possible by a loving family, deep friendships, a supportive religion, and (perhaps most of all) a hope for a better life. This sense of hope was not a product of war but was rather the core of his being.

Once the war was over, his hopefulness invigorated his faith in religion and love for family life, helping him to bring five children into the world, and to travel the globe educating audiences of adults and schoolchildren about his inspirational story of survival.

For many Jews, including my father, threats to their lives during the Holocaust were so formidable that, no matter how actively they tried to resist these perils, survival often depended on assistance from courageous people outside of the Jewish community. We know of at least 22,000 such rescuers because they have been officially recognized for their actions by Yad Vashem. It is also important to note that an unknown number of non-Jewish individuals certainly tried in secret to save Jews but were never honored publicly for their efforts because either recognition was never sought or the rescue effort failed. The risks were particularly high in Nazi-occupied Poland, where the German authorities widely threatened to kill anyone assisting Jews and carried out this penalty against at least 704 non-Jews.[2] At a time when many others tried to save only themselves, the extraordinary rescuers made a different choice. They put their lives—and often the lives of their family and neighbors—at risk to protect their fellow human beings and thus became heroes in the truest sense.

I will never know exactly why individuals like Maria and Michał Mazurek—the Polish Catholic farmers who gave shelter to my father and my uncle Symcha after their escape from Sobibór—decided to save en-dangered strangers. Perhaps they were motivated by deeply held religious convictions. Or maybe they were motivated by a sense of personal obliga-tion to their neighbor. But I prefer to think that the Mazureks risked their lives to save others because something in them simply said: we must.

Today most of us could save lives—both in our own communities and in faraway places—without risking our own. No matter how daunting the challenge, we can and must devote our energies to eliminating the often-interrelated scourges of hunger, disease, environmental degradation, war, and genocide. To paraphrase the Mishnah, we are not required to complete the task, yet we are not free to withdraw from it. And we can find inspira-tion in the striking examples of the Mazureks' righteousness, the Sobibór conspirators' bravery, and my father's sheer resilience.

On the other hand, we must always strive to learn from the Holocaust's enormous manifestations of evil and indifference. Too many of us avoid exposing ourselves to vivid depictions of pain and suffering. It is only natural to turn away in revulsion. But disengaging from the reality of what occurred not so long ago in modern-day Europe is fraught with danger, for it can precipitate one's own involvement in injustices such as genocide—as either a victim, a bystander, or a perpetrator.

Unless we allow ourselves to vicariously experience a measure of the pain and inspiration of a child survivor of genocide such as my father, we will never fully learn from our shared history, and we will never stop hatred, violence, and injustice from happening again and again. With this book, my father and I hope to have contributed something of value to this struggle.

JOSEPH BIALOWITZ

A Promise at Sobibór

1

Before War

Our hour of religious study has just ended. I attend a small, Polish public school comprised of roughly equal numbers of Catholic and Jewish students. Along with my Jewish classmates, we share the same teachers and study the same subjects as the Catholic students, but in different classrooms. The only difference in the curriculum comes during the "religious hour." A revered priest teaches the Catholic schoolchildren about Catholicism, while two local Jewish women, Hadassa and Grincza, teach us about Judaism. I never know exactly what the Catholic children learn during their religion class, but judging from my vantage point on the soccer field, where I now stand with Motel and Josele, today's lesson must have been quite unusual: a small group of yelling boys bursts out from the schoolhouse, throwing stones, accusing us of murder, and telling us to go to a place that most of us would give anything to get to, especially at this moment: "Christ killers! Jews to Palestine!"

For a thirteen-year-old boy, I am only of average build—about five and one-half feet tall and 130 pounds—but am able to fight back against the slightly older boy who attacks me. I manage to gain the upper hand, but two reinforcements arrive and shove me to the ground. My other schoolmates stand helplessly to the side, watching with looks of pity in their faces. The bullies beat me until I bleed. At last the nightmare ends when one of my favorite teachers, Mr. Śliwa, arrives. He pulls my attackers away and reproaches them sternly. "This is no way to act! Now go home!" The boys run off. "I'm very sorry, Fiszel," says Mr. Śliwa. "You know that these are just a few troublemakers."

With some help from Mr. Śliwa, I pick myself up and find Motel and Josele. Motel is taller and stronger than me, while Josele is on the small side. But strength is of no matter: none of us has escaped without scrapes, cuts, bruises, and torn clothes. "We need to get out of here," I say.

We live in Izbica Lubelski, a quiet but lively town of about six thousand people on the main road between the small cities of Zamość and Krasnystaw and on the railroad line connecting the large cities of Warsaw and Lwów. It is full of adjoined ramshackle homes, unpaved roads, basic shops, and a market square, all built on generally flat land surrounded by hills, forests, and farms. Winters are cold, dark, and snowy; summers are hot, humid, and often filled with mosquitoes. Most of the townspeople are Jews whose families, including my mother's, have lived in Izbica for centuries. In the early nineteenth century, Izbica had spawned a famous sect of Hasidic Jews known as the Izhbitz Hasidim. In recent years Hasidism has begun to give way to a more modern outlook in Izbica. Though about two-thirds of the town's Jews (including my family) do not dress in the traditional black garb of the Hasidic Jews, we still uphold the traditions of the Jewish faith, especially by observing the Sabbath and eating only *kasher* foods.[1] The few Jews who do consume pork must be prepared for the repercussions: my father has recently barred me from spending time with one of my friends because his family is known to eat the forbidden meat.

Only about nine hundred of the townspeople are Poles. In the neighboring villages and farms, though, it's the opposite: almost no Jews, but several thousand Poles. In the schools, shops, and markets, we all assemble to deal with each other, but otherwise we interact very seldom. Centuries of living like this, in basic separation from and habitual suspicion of the other, has helped breed a kind of comfortable resentment between us and them. Only occasionally has the resentment turned as violent as it has today. And despite our religious differences, I know we are all countrymen.

I am a Polish Jew. I speak Yiddish, but I also know the Polish language because I learn it at school and speak it with my friends and neighbors who are Poles. For four days each week, I go after school for several hours to a small *heder* where since the age of five I have learned how to read, write, and pray in Hebrew, and where I am now studying the traditional Jewish texts and their commentaries.[2] But I also enjoy my public school classes about Polish history and government. There is even a story told by my parents that the great leader of the Polish struggle for independence, Józef Piłsudski, once lodged at our house for a night. Some of my favorite times of the year are the Jewish holidays, when our whole family comes together for festive meals. Yet I also look forward to the Polish national holidays, when bands play colorful, marching music in the streets. Every year on Independence Day, Mr. Śliwa leads all the Jewish students to synagogue to pray for the Polish government.

But my friends and I are intent on finding better lives than the ones we have in Izbica. We look forward to someday moving to a more modern place with less poverty and greater opportunities. The only question is how. "Where would we go?" asks Josele, as he nurses a bloody hand. "To Palestine, where we will be able to live just like everyone else in the world," I answer. "I wouldn't mind getting to Zamość if I had the money for a bus ticket," he says.

Josele's circumstances are similar to those of about 90 percent of the Jews in Izbica. They are so poor as to make absurd the idea of paying for a move to Palestine or even the closest city. After they satisfy their day-to-day needs, they simply thank God. Most of Izbica's Jews, especially the Hasidic Jews, live near the government-owned brick-making factory called the *klinkiernia*, but only Poles are allowed to work there. What few material possessions Izbica's Jews have are usually earned by selling all manner of inexpensive necessities in tiny shops, peddling goods at the weekly open-air market, or laboring in the flour mills, the sugar refinery, and the sawmill. Despite their efforts Izbica's poor are often forced to depend on the charity of others.

Although my family is not wealthy, we are fairly prominent within the town and live more comfortably than most of our neighbors. My father, Szyja, who is originally from the nearby town of Siedliszcze, owns a small tannery, where he produces mostly shoe leather. With his modest earnings, he has been able to send my two older brothers, Symcha and Jakub, ages twenty-seven and twenty-four, to school in Warsaw. They have done well, with Symcha finding work in Warsaw as a representative of our town's pharmacy and Jakub obtaining a position as an electrical engineer. Despite their relative success and comfort in Warsaw, however, even my brothers feel deep inside that there is little hope for us in Poland and that only in Palestine can we have a decent future.

As we walk home, my friends and I continue discussing our hopes. Everyone around us has unique ideas about how to improve our situation, but first and foremost we admire the people who have simply made it out. These lucky and resourceful few have emigrated to countries as far away as Brazil and Palestine. On the days when they departed from town, large cheering crowds had gathered at our small train station to bid them farewell and wish them good luck in their journey.

Their achievements have inspired us all the more to follow in their footsteps. Young people all over Izbica are studying foreign languages, including Hebrew, Russian, Spanish, and Esperanto. Many people are also devoted to political movements, of which there are all shades of groups from which to choose: Zionist, Socialist, and others. Both of my older brothers are Socialists and Zionists who have applied for emigration to Palestine, but they have not yet succeeded because of strict quotas imposed by the British government. Symcha and Jakub support David Ben Gurion's Poaley Syjon group.[3]

Many young Zionists, including Jakub and boys and girls from all over Poland, are preparing for emigration to Palestine and life on a *kibbutz* by performing physical labor inside and outside Izbica in *hachsharah* groups.[4] Most of these groups have members between the ages of sixteen and thirty. I can't wait to be old enough to join one of the hachsharahs. In his group, Jakub and his friends have learned to milk cows. They also chop wood for lower wages than are received by other workers. From what little I know of Palestine's geography, I am skeptical of how much wood chopping is really necessary there. But the boys and girls of the hachsharahs are happy to gain the work experience. A popular saying among them is: "What a joy, what a pleasure, to cut wood for a gentile."[5]

Because of a slowdown in business at the Belgian company where he works in Warsaw, Jakub has returned to Izbica to help many of the outsiders adjust to their new lives in the local hachsharahs. He has been in Izbica since the beginning of the summer, spending much of his time away from home, delivering lectures about Zionism to the members of the hachsharahs. I admire Jakub's idealism and commitment to his beliefs. However, unlike both Jakub and Symcha, I support Zeev Jabotinsky's "Revisionist" Zionist group and so does my friend Motel.[6] A year ago we both had walked to a field on the outskirts of Izbica to hear an inspiring lecture by Jabotinsky himself. He was traveling throughout Poland, from place to place, urging crowds of Jewish people to organize, go to Palestine, and fight against the British to create a Jewish state, because we had little future in Poland besides oppression and poverty. On the day that we saw Jabotinsky, he had implored us, "Jews, learn to shoot!"

Motel and I try to convince Josele that Jabotinsky offers us the soundest alternative. "We need to live in our own country if we are ever to be truly safe and free," I say as we head into town. "But Jews have never achieved anything without struggle," adds Motel, "and in Palestine it will be no different." "Right," I say, "the British will never give us our land on a silver platter!" "So what are you guys saying?" asks Josele. "That we should run away to Palestine and form a Jewish army there?" "Yes!" I answer. "We'll be known as the elite Izbica commandos, trained to protect all Jewish schoolchildren in Palestine and around the world!"

I am truly willing to fight for Palestine if only I can find a way to get there. I've even tried to participate in Jabotinsky's youth movement, known as Betar. Along with Motel, I have attended a few meetings of the group's Izbica chapter and been impressed by the confident, optimistic spirit shared by all the members. However, Symcha and Jakub will not let me join officially, telling me that Betar is a bunch of "fascists." Indeed, members of my brothers' Poaley Syjon group have been involved in several scuffles with the often overzealous Betar members. Out of respect for my brothers, I have chosen not to join the movement, although I continue to support the group's ideology.

Having walked along the road for five minutes or so, my friends and I are now in the center of town. On any other day, we might stop at the soda shop to flirt with the girls or visit the movie house. But this is Friday afternoon, and everyone is hastily preparing for the Sabbath. My first errand is to pick up my father's repaired watch. So we enter the watchmaker's shop owned by Jan Schultz, a tall, thin man known all over town not just for being the watchmaker but also for being of German ancestry. Despite the terrible things we have heard about the treatment of Jews within Germany,

Mr. Schultz has continued to act kindly and politely to our family and to everyone else. We speak with him in Polish, although when I pay him for the watch, he smiles and thanks me in German, "Danke schoen."

On our way to the bakery where Josele needs to purchase *challah* for his family's Sabbath meal, we spot my Aunt Chana, whose husband, Ichak, is my mother's brother and a well-respected textile merchant in town.[7] Aunt Chana is going around town distributing packages of food to the many people who are too poor to provide for their own Sabbath meal. The charitable spirit is strong throughout my family. My father often donates money for my aunt to purchase this food, and he gives interest-free loans to support some of the town's neediest Jews. This is all part of the widespread practice of *tzedaka* in Izbica.[8]

Of all the people in my family, Aunt Chana is the one I can least afford to encounter at this moment. She has a penchant for worrying about the smallest things. I know that if Aunt Chana sees me in my current condition, she will worry herself sick. Even worse, she will make sure that my mother becomes worried sick, too. Maybe Aunt Chana will even convince my mother to keep me in the house for my own protection! So I take care to stand behind Motel. Luckily she continues making her deliveries without spotting me.

After the close call with Aunt Chana, we enter the bakery, where Josele places his order for the challah that his family will eat during the Sabbath. The baker has just removed the golden, sweet-smelling loaf from the large brick oven. My mouth waters as he hands two loaves of the warm bread to Josele. But I knew that even tastier challah, baked by my mother, awaits me at home. We say "Gut shabbes" to one another and split off in the directions of our respective houses.[9]

I arrive battered and bruised back at home. My mother, Bajla, drops everything when she sees me. "What happened to you, my *kindel*?" she asks immediately.[10] After telling her all about the fight, I can see from the pained expression on my mother's face that maybe I have revealed too much. So I try to cheer her up. "At least Aunt Chana didn't see me!" I say. My joke tells my mother that I'm OK. She goes right to work, first treating my cuts, then giving me some ice to apply to my swollen eye. I hope to one day study medicine so that, like my older brothers, I can be part of a profession that improves people's lives. So I enjoy the opportunity to learn from the loving way in which my mother tends to me. But I am still dwelling on the conversation I have just had with my friends. "Why does everyone hate us so much?" I ask.

"This is how we live here, Fiszele.[11] It has been like this for hundreds of years. But remember, he who can't endure the bad will not live to see the good."

Her answer doesn't satisfy me. "Why don't you complain to the principal of the school?" I ask.

"I did the last time. The principal said she would look into it."

My mother is more prominent in Izbica than most other women, so if she cannot convince the principal to intervene, nobody's mother can. During the thirty years since she married my father at the age of eighteen, my mother has devoted herself not only to family life but to the life of the community. Her stature in the community stems from several roles that she plays in Izbica. For the few women who are illiterate, my mother recites the prayers aloud during the Sabbath and holiday services. Any word my mother utters within the synagogue, dozens of voices repeat.

Furthermore, each significant Jewish town in Poland typically has at least a few families who have been the trusted bakers of the Passover *matze* for generations.[12] In Izbica one of these families is the Klyds, from which are descended my mother and her four siblings: Ichak, Szlome, Cira, and Czypa. (Uncle Szlome had cut his hand and died from the resulting infection a few years ago, leaving behind four children—Sara, Rachel, Ichak, and Alter—and my Aunt Zlata, who had died shortly thereafter of cancer.)

My mother and her two sisters have inherited our home because they are responsible for continuing the operation of its magnificently large oven. Every spring many people depend on our family and our oven to provide them with matze. My family always approaches the matze-baking process not as a job by which to earn money but rather as an honor. Baking the matze allows us to help others to observe the Jewish tradition. We provide matze to everyone in Izbica at little or no cost, depending on his or her means. The large scale of the operation also means that for the four weeks before the annual holiday, our home is overrun by about twenty of Izbica's prettiest young girls, handpicked by my mother to assist in the meticulous baking process. Whenever my older brothers return from Warsaw to celebrate the holiday with us, they are certainly not bothered by the presence of all these girls (though Symcha wants to become a successful pharmacist before getting married). I, who am only beginning to appreciate my mother's ulterior motives, tend to focus more intently on my assigned roles. As a small boy I had started off by adding flour to the dough. When I got a little older, I had graduated to pouring the water into the dough. Most recently I have been promoted to the position of poking the holes in the unbaked matze. My dream is to eventually achieve the highest responsibility of all: inserting and removing the delicate matze from the oven in accordance with the strict laws of *kashrus*.[13]

But today our kitchen is alive with just as much activity as before Passover. Because of the special, large brick oven that we have in our kitchen, our family serves another important role for the Jewish community: people use our oven to keep their containers of stew warm during the Sabbath. Every Friday afternoon women from all over town walk to our house to place their pots full of delicious *chollent* in our oven.[14] The women then return after the synagogue services to pick up these warm delights, which form the basis of everyone's Sabbath meals.

When sundown arrives, the beautiful rhythms of the Sabbath begin. Our family normally welcomes the Sabbath with a long dinner in our modest home. Because of my father's relative success in business, our house is of a slightly higher standard than most others in town. Constructed of wood, it has two bedrooms in addition to a living room, a kitchen, and an attic. My oldest sister, Rywka, occupies one of the bedrooms with her husband and their two young children, Josele and Sara. At thirty years old, she is tall and thin, very attractive, and a dedicated mother who also helps my mother a great deal with household chores. Her husband is not as religious as my family, but everyone gets along.

I share the other bedroom with my parents and my sister Toba. She is sixteen years old, and because of her blonde hair, blue eyes, and outgoing personality, all the boys of Izbica want to date her. With her kind and compassionate nature, she is dreaming of becoming a teacher one day. My other sister, Brancha, who at eighteen resembles Toba and is just as attractive, had gone to Warsaw after the seventh grade to live with Symcha and Jakub.

She hasn't decided what to study yet, but she is working as a seamstress and saving money prior to beginning her studies. Izbica's girls are just as educated as its boys in both secular and religious subjects, but there are few jobs for women outside the home unless they venture beyond our small town. Since returning from Warsaw, Jakub has been using our attic as his bedroom. In the same attic, several years earlier, our father had caught Jakub eating ham and scolded my brother severely. The last important occupant of our house is our pet cat, who enjoys splitting her time between the interior of the house and the backyard, where our few chickens can keep her company.

We also had a brother named Chaim who died before I was born. When he was only six years old, he had been run over by a horse-drawn cart onto which he had tried to jump just after it had begun moving. My parents speak often of how precocious Chaim had been and how, when I was younger, I had reminded them of him. Whenever they talk about little Chaim, I can sense the pain caused by my brother's untimely death. This anguish, I know, will always be a part of our family. At the same time, the memory of Chaim also inspires us to care for and protect one another all the more.

This evening my Aunt Czypa and her daughter, Hena, have joined us for dinner. A few years ago, Czypa's husband had abandoned his family and left for America. Ever since then Czypa has supported herself and her daughter by working as a peddler. For days at a time, she travels through the nearby villages pushing a cart full of surplus textiles that she receives on consignment from my uncle Ichak, who is a successful merchant. She goes door to door and barters with the farmers for fruits, vegetables, and poultry. Then she returns to Izbica and sells them in the outdoor marketplace. Czypa is one of the few women in Izbica who is forced to fend for herself in this way. We all feel sorry for her. But she is a strong woman who has never once complained.

Though we don't practice the traditions of the Hasidic Jews, on the Sabbath we often host visiting Hasidic rabbis because my father is considered one of the leaders of the community. Our family's dinner guest this evening is a rabbi from the town of Radzyń. I can easily identify his affiliation with a quick glance at the unusually colored *tzitzis* that he wears: whereas nearly all Jewish men wear white tzitzis, he dons the hallmark blue tzitzis of the Hasidic Jews from Radzyń and Izbica.[15]

The Sabbath dinner consists of gefilte fish, homemade horseradish, chicken noodle soup, chicken, *flanken, simmis, kugel,* compote, apple strudel, and—my absolute favorite food from my mother's kitchen— *ruggelach.*[16] She uses just the right amount of sweet cheese and always finds the tastiest berries to use for the jam that fills the inside of the tiny, rolled pastries. I look forward to her ruggelach all week and always make sure to save room for them.

Between blessings and songs, we debate politics and how to remain safe. Schoolyard bullies are the least of our worries. Everyone knows that economic conditions in Poland had been very difficult throughout the long foreign occupation that began in 1795 and ended in 1918. Since Poland gained independence, life has continued to be difficult for everyone in the country thanks to the destruction and hardship wrought by the World War, the Polish–Bolshevik War that followed it, and the worldwide Great Depression. We still cannot trust that the Soviet Union, led by the power-hungry Stalin, will not invade us again. And Hitler's Germany has invaded our peaceful neighbor to the south, Czechoslovakia, and seems eager to expand German territory even more. We all wonder if Germany will invade Poland next and what that would mean for us as Polish Jews. We know that German Jews have been the victims of discriminatory laws and deadly pogroms: *Kristallnacht* had occurred nine months ago, in November 1938.[17] And I cannot forget the first time that I heard one of Hitler's speeches. Standing with dozens of other people in front of the candy store, we had listened to a radio broadcast that we didn't entirely comprehend, but the German language's similarity to Yiddish had allowed me to understand enough to know that Hitler was blaming the *Juden* for all of Germany's problems.[18] Moreover, I had not needed to know any German to sense the rage in his voice.

Though surely our guest rabbi is himself fearful of the future, he tries to calm everyone by reminding us that God once brought us out from Egypt "with a mighty hand." God, the rabbi assures us, will again deliver us from harm. The rabbi's belief that God will determine human events surprises me not one bit, because it is a doctrine that is well known in

Izbica. The founder of Izbica's Hasidic Jews, Rabbi Mordechaj Josef Leiner, had been the first rabbi to teach that "all is in the hands of Heaven including reverence for Heaven."[19] This faith in God's will had surely protected Jews from despair during difficult times. But I know from Jewish history classes that there are many examples of Jews who had not relied only on divine assistance. Heroes such as Juda Makabi and Mordechaj had used both their might and their wisdom to fight for the survival of the Jewish people. I consider telling the rabbi that sometimes reverence for God means battling to save the life that God has given us. I also want to tell him that in heder I have learned that the Talmud says, "If someone comes to kill you, rise up and kill him (first)."[20] But it would not be polite for a boy to argue with such an esteemed rabbi. And besides, even if we choose to fight for our lives, what good would it do if—in spite of Jabotinsky's encouragement—almost none of us own guns or know how to shoot them? So I just keep quiet and help myself to as much of my mother's delicious cooking as possible.

The next morning, we walk together to the synagogue. Constructed of dark wood, it is Izbica's tallest and most beautiful building. Each week one thousand people pack into the synagogue for the morning service on the Sabbath day. This means that it's also a very good place to socialize. When we step past the ornate black iron gate that opens onto the front yard of the synagogue, I find dozens of younger children playing, while the older girls and boys are already busy flirting. But I'm not concerned with flirting anymore, because I have a beautiful girlfriend. Her name is Sima. We have strong feelings for each other. She is the best student in school, excelling especially at math, which makes her dream of becoming an accountant one day in a larger town than Izbica. We have been dating since last winter, which we had enjoyed very much together by going sleigh riding down the hills surrounding Izbica whenever we could. We are happy every second that we are together. In school I always share my cheese sandwiches with her because she loves the freshly baked, sweet challah rolls that my mother prepares. In return I eat her egg salad sandwiches on rye bread, which I enjoy as well.

Since Sima is also religious, she is at the synagogue. All the women sit in a balcony behind the men, so that the men won't be distracted from their prayers. But as is my custom, I peek into the women's section and wave hello to Sima. Here I see my mother reading the Hebrew prayers aloud to the few women who cannot read.

The *chazzan* chants the Torah beautifully.[21] I love to sing at synagogue, especially during the annual High Holy Day services, when I am allowed with several other young people to ascend the *bimah* to sing a prayer alongside the chazzan.[22] These holidays are now fast approaching, and in anticipation of the big day, for the last few weeks I have been playfully annoying my sister by loudly practicing my singing role at home.

The revered spiritual leader of Izbica's Jewish community is Rabbi Elijahu Landau. His thoughtful words are always full of wisdom. My father and I feel fortunate whenever we can sit next to Rabbi Landau in the synagogue. Often we are guests for Sabbath dinner at Rabbi Landau's house. On some occasions we are even privileged to have him visit our home. For example, every year Rabbi Landau leads a delegation of rabbis who come to our house to inspect our matze-baking process and ensure that it is completely kasher. He is a very close friend of our family whom we—as well as less religious Jews and even a few Poles—turn to for guidance on all kinds of questions, large or small. My mother was once preparing a chicken when she found a blemish that had not looked right. She had instructed me to bring the chicken to Rabbi Landau's house so that he could tell us if the chicken was still kasher. He had taken the chicken and, like a doctor, carefully examined all its parts for fifteen minutes. Then Rabbi Landau had pinched my cheeks and pronounced with a smile: "Fiszele, go home and tell your mother that she can cook the chicken."

2

War Begins

On September 1, 1939, the radio in our living room brings the news we have feared would come: the Germans have invaded western Poland. We guess it will be at least several days before the fighting can possibly reach our town in the eastern part of the country. Meanwhile, we worry most about the fates of Symcha and Brancha in Warsaw, whom we now have no way to contact.

Over the next few days, we spend many hours huddled around the radio with our neighbors, many of whom do not have one of their own. We all hope that the brave Polish army will be able to fend off the German invasion. But the reports are not encouraging. The Germans seem to be gaining ground, steadily getting closer to Izbica. Our anxiety grows.

Finally it begins: the war comes to Izbica. First, we hear the roar of German warplanes above. We all take shelter in the house, except for Jakub, who is catching up with one of his old friends on the other side of town. Then we hear and feel bombs and artillery exploding around the outskirts of the city, where there must be Polish defense forces stationed. We silently pray that the Polish army, with God's help, will prevail. But we know that Germany's military might is overwhelming. Toba is crying.

Within just a few hours of the bombardment, we watch from our windows as the first German troops enter our city, dressed in clean uniforms and sparkling helmets. Not even in films have I ever seen a German soldier before. They are worse than I imagined. Walking in formation and carrying their guns while singing German war songs, the soldiers are simply terrifying to behold.

Jakub returns to the house, much to everyone's relief. But he is visibly shaken. He also smells like farm animals. "When we heard the planes, we ran to the fields outside town because we thought it would be safer," Jakub says. "We hid in a barn. But there must have been Polish fighters nearby, because the planes started firing on the barn. Bullets were streaming in through the roof. Several of the animals in the barn were hit."

This must have been especially difficult for Jakub because he cares greatly for animals. In fact, he may never have chosen to become an electrician had it not been for the electrified fence that he had built while still a teenager to protect his pet pigeons from the thieves who once tried to steal them.

The next day my father ventures out to check on his tannery. When he returns that night, his long gray beard is gone. "They cut it," says my father matter-of-factly. "The Germans."

Some soldiers had grabbed my father while he was walking down the street and had cut off what, for them, is one of the main physical symbols of a pious Jewish man. My father says that he has seen several Hasidic Jews walking around without beards and *payes*.[1] They, too, had been unfortunate enough to cross paths with German troops. My father certainly feels humiliated, but having heard the stories of deadly attacks on Jews in Germany, we are just thankful he has not been killed. Later that night, however, we learn that others have not been so lucky: Jakub brings news from his friends that at least six Jews, including the butcher, have been murdered by German soldiers.

Our town has experienced a pogrom.

The following day we mourn at the synagogue and hold funerals for the dead. But we try not to despair. Had not Jews before us experienced such attacks? Over the centuries our people have learned to live with these terrible but isolated massacres. Life always returns to normal eventually. On the other hand, we need to brace ourselves for further violence. In fact we have to expect the worst that we can imagine. We are in the middle of a war zone, where people will act unpredictably, even violently. And if Kristallnacht has occurred in Germany and we are now occupied by Germany, then who knows what tomorrow will bring?

To make matters worse, we still have not heard any news from Symcha and Brancha since the Germans have invaded Poland. Then, just a few days later, an unmarked Polish military jeep pulls up to our house and out jump my brother and sister. Everyone is relieved to know that they are safe. Many hugs and kisses are exchanged before they have a chance to explain to us how they have managed to come back to Izbica.

Symcha says he had been walking down a street in Warsaw when he heard a voice calling out, "Symcha, Symcha!" The voice was that of a Polish soldier whom Symcha had grown up with in Izbica. The soldier had told Symcha that he was going to drive back to Izbica in the unmarked military jeep that he possessed. But the man had been worried about what could happen if Germans stopped him along the way home. Knowing that Symcha's knowledge of Yiddish would allow him to communicate in German as well, the soldier had asked if Symcha would be willing to come along to serve as an interpreter. Symcha had immediately agreed, on the condition that he could also bring Brancha. The deal had been struck. When they began the journey, they had agreed that if they were stopped by Germans, Symcha would simply explain that they were all civilians driving home to Izbica. Fortunately, they have made it all the way back without being stopped even once.

Everyone is happy to have the family together again during these uncertain days. I'm also happy to have them back simply because Symcha and Brancha, as well as Jakub, are my older siblings and I look up to them. Growing up in such a small house, we had all been very close with one another. We had done many things together, such as helping our mother bake the matze every year and helping our father operate the tannery. Often we had performed songs together in the back of our house for our parents and other relatives. My mother had always loved when we sang "Majn Jidysze Mame" for her.[2] Brancha, who is an excellent artist, had loved teaching me how to paint. Symcha had always found time to help me with my schoolwork. Each Saturday night, Symcha had taught dance classes that were always filled with his friends and other young adults. I was always too young to participate in the classes, but sometimes Symcha had allowed me to attend as an observer. Tango, foxtrot, and waltz had been his specialties. Everyone had been in awe when they watched him dance. It had made me proud to know that my brother was such an excellent dance teacher.

Even after moving to Warsaw, Symcha and Brancha had always brought us warm coats and beautiful clothes whenever they came home to visit. But

I would have traded all these gifts just for the chance to live with them again. Now they are back, and it appears that they will stay for a long time. Our house is sure to be much more fun than it has been without them.

The next day the German soldiers inexplicably retreat from Izbica, and the Soviet Union's troops soon arrive. We don't trust the Soviets because they are Germany's allies and they have joined in the invasion of Poland. However, judging from the earlier pogrom perpetrated by the Germans, we believe that we'll be no worse off under Soviet control than under German control. On the other hand, our town's few Communist Party activists—there are probably fewer than five in total—must be happy with the change.

The Soviets do not seem to trouble us. Life returns to normal. But just a few weeks later, around the end of September, the Soviets abruptly begin leaving Izbica. It is apparent that there has been another change. We fear that the Germans will be back to reoccupy the town. As the Soviet soldiers retreat toward the east, some townspeople follow them. Life in Russia will surely be difficult and dangerous, but these people apparently prefer the devil they know to the devil they don't know.

With the retreat nearly complete, Jakub enters the house and announces that he and one of his friends from the electrical trade have decided to flee to the Soviet Union.

"What is your plan?" asks my very concerned father.

"We'll find our cousins in Ludman," answers Jakub, referring to the town just across the nearby Bug River where our Uncle Ichak and Aunt Chana's daughter, Lea, lives with her husband. "We'll bring money and buy tickets to go wherever it is safest in the Soviet Union. And I'm sure I can find work wherever we end up."

I can see the worry on my father's face. Jakub is his son. But he is not a child anymore. My father has no choice but to respect my brother's decision. After Jakub collects his belongings into a small bag, we all give him a good-bye kiss. He promises to write after arriving in the Soviet Union.

"Jakub, there is one more thing you must promise to do," says my father. "Once you are outside Izbica, recite the Prayer for Travelers. I have written the words for you."[3] Despite Jakub's lack of religious conviction and his previous differences with our father, Jakub promises to recite the prayer. We all hug him. And then he is gone.

For several weeks the town is in a kind of no-man's land, occupied by neither Germans nor Soviets. During this uncertain period, lawlessness becomes evident. A grenade is thrown into the busy outdoor marketplace, killing several Jews. Apparently someone has felt justified in carrying out this indiscriminate attack against Jews because some prominent Communists are Jews, and it is possible that a few of Izbica's Jews have assisted the Soviet authorities in Izbica. Doubts about the patriotism of Polish Jews may also have been raised by the scenes of Jews like my brother Jakub, who are not Communists, leaving Izbica to seek refuge in the enemy territory of the Soviet Union.

When the Germans return, they bring order with them. Their military policemen patrol the town and ensure that everyone goes peaceably about his or her daily business.[4] On Saturday evenings the streets of Izbica are filled with young people socializing. Despite the war the atmosphere on these nights is festive. For these special occasions, I dress up in my very fashionable *tompehoizen*, which Brancha has brought me from Warsaw.[5] I am the only boy in town who walks around in these unique pants. But I do not at all mind standing out. The only important thing is that Sima always smiles when she sees me in these pants. She tells me that I am the best dresser in all Izbica.

The Germans begin declaring special rules for Jews. One of the first decrees is an order for Jews to wear a Star of David at all times.[6] We wear them on white armbands that we place over our sleeves. Putting on a Star of David for the first time feels very difficult because we know that identification will allow the Germans to persecute us more easily.

The Germans also stop the public schooling of Jews. My parents respond by immediately arranging a private tutor for me and Toba. Education has always been paramount in my family. Often the first question my father asks at the dinner table is "Did you get any perfect scores today on your tests?" Even in the middle of a war, my parents expect us not to neglect our studies.

Our new tutor is a tall, religious man with a long beard. He is an experienced heder teacher so he knows how to instruct us on Jewish religion and culture. But he also teaches other subjects, such as philosophy and mathematics. My father pays him with leather that can be used to make shoes. Our classes are held about three times a week for two hours each day. Although the lessons are brief, we learn much in those few hours. It helps to take our minds off the war. Naturally I am also happy not to have to attend school all day anymore. But I miss my friends and the less restricted life we had led before the war began.

In the winter things start to become more difficult. Jews from western Poland begin flowing into our district. About one thousand Jews arrive and are given shelter in Jewish homes around Izbica. The assignments are made by the newly formed *Judenrat*, which is comprised of prominent local Jews.[7] Among the Judenrat members are several business owners, but not my father. They have been appointed to their positions by Schultz. Though he had been a watchmaker before the war, Schultz's status as a *Volksdeutscher* under German law has helped to earn him an appointment as the new mayor of Izbica.[8] He is openly collaborating with the German occupiers.

We don't house any of the new families because around the same time that they have arrived, a family—the mother, the father, and two boys aged eight and ten—at whose home Symcha and Jakub had boarded before the war has fled the new Jewish ghetto in Warsaw in order to stay with us. They had felt it would be safer in Izbica than in Warsaw, and they had also thought that it would be easier to find food. We give them whatever we can.

The Germans put many people to work for them in some way. My father is allowed to operate his tannery, but all the finished leather must go to the German war effort and he is paid only with food. I help by carrying heavy pails full of water from the well to the tannery. The Germans also periodically call upon the Judenrat to supply dozens of people at a time for various work groups. It is easy for the Judenrat to find volunteers because the poorest people of Izbica see it as a chance to be fed in exchange for their labor. Teenagers like me also volunteer because the small rations of salami, sardines, and cigarettes with which the Germans pay us are easy for us to sell and thus obtain spending money for ourselves. Because I am young and strong, I volunteer to shovel snow on the main road leading through town. Along with other boys, including my friends Jankiel and Mojsze, we shovel huge amounts of snow nearly every day for several weeks. The snow drifts are even higher than our heads. Schultz supervises us.

One day we are ordered to hand over all our jewelry to the Judenrat. We comply with the order, thinking it will give us a better chance of surviving.

Schultz arrives at our home to personally confiscate the jewelry. We give him enough to make him happy and hide our remaining valuables.

By early 1940 fleeing to the Soviet Union seems increasingly like a reasonable choice. The German occupation extends only to the Bug River some thirty miles away. The river is not closely guarded. We have heard that on the other side one can live in Soviet-occupied Poland without fearing additional German decrees against the Jews. However, we still have not received any word from Jakub. Symcha decides to leave Izbica to cross the river and determine if it would be safe for the rest of the family to follow. His plan is to go to the town of Ludman to meet up with Cousin Lea, her husband, and, hopefully, Jakub.

After a few weeks, Symcha returns with news that he had successfully crossed the river. He says the journey was fairly easy and life on the other side of the river was safe. Cousin Lea and her husband are still in Ludman. They are OK, but they do not know Jakub's whereabouts. Now, Symcha says, he has come back to Izbica to bring whoever he can with him this time. Everyone agrees that for now he should take Brancha on the journey. The following day they depart together. But just a few days later, they return to the house. They say it has now become too dangerous to cross the river.

With the arrival of the warmer spring months, the Germans begin calling upon the Judenrat to supply yet more volunteers for the various work groups. The father of the Warsaw family staying with us is sent each day to a field near Zamość to help build an airstrip. He returns every night utterly exhausted and, after quickly eating something, goes straight to sleep in the attic, which he shares with his family. Soon, instead of returning in the evenings, the man and the other volunteers are often gone for weeks at a time. They are being sent to work camps. They report that living conditions in the camps are even more difficult than in Izbica, with people forced to perform heavy labor and sleep in crowded quarters. Not surprisingly, the supply of volunteers dwindles. So the Germans begin forcing the Judenrat to assign people to work. It becomes a relief not to be called.

One day the Judenrat delivers orders for Symcha to work on an irrigation project about six miles outside Izbica. But we know that his skills as a pharmacist are needed in Izbica. So my parents approach the Judenrat and request that I replace him. Permission is granted, and I am brought by truck to the project. Everyone is worried about me, but Symcha tells me, "Don't worry. We'll get you out soon."

I spend a few weeks digging irrigation ditches with people from Izbica and some other towns, such as Zamość. I am probably the youngest person in the group. Among the people from my town is Jankiel Pelc, a close friend of the family. They give us barely anything to eat, but I am lucky to be among the people whose family at home has enough money to send extra packages of food. Fortunately, the Germans allow us to receive these packages. We sleep in military barracks. It's the first time I have slept anywhere but home. It feels strange at first, but I adjust quickly. Besides, it is even a bit nice to be treated like an adult. After a few weeks, the Judenrat arranges for me to return to Izbica.

When I get home, my parents tell me that they have gone to the Judenrat and used their influence to help get me out. "Did you pay for my release?" I ask my father. He ignores my question. If my father does not want to tell me what price he had to pay, it must have been quite costly. Simply happy to be home, I drop the subject.

Soon people fail to respond to even the mandatory work assignments issued by the Judenrat. The supply of Jewish volunteers for the difficult work details runs completely dry. It is then that we witness our first *akcja*.[9] I am walking down the street one afternoon when I hear a commotion around the corner. Truckloads of Germans are looking for workers and grabbing any able-bodied men they can find. I run inside the *Bejt Jaakow*, where some women quickly hide me inside a closet.[10] One of the teachers, Mrs. Schwarcz, then goes to tell my family that I am there. About two hours later, after it appears that the roundup is over, Brancha and Toba come to the closet bearing a wig and a girl's dress for me to wear for the walk home. As I put on the dress, I remember the happier times when the Purim holiday would approach and my family would dress me up in costume. Last year I had paraded around town dressed as a Hasidic rabbi. That costume is exactly the opposite of the disguise I now need. I return home without incident, happy that Sima has not seen me.

When I arrive at our house, I discover that Rywka's husband has been caught in the roundups. My father has also learned from members of the Judenrat that Izbica's most prominent non-Jews, including several doctors and two schoolteachers, have been taken away. One of them is the kind-hearted Mr. Śliwa. The second teacher, Mr. Podgórski, had been another of my favorites. Both had always taken an interest in me and my brothers, and after Symcha and Jakub had left for Warsaw these teachers had often asked me how my brothers were faring. Now they are gone. Their arrests make it all the more clear that the Germans will stop at nothing to solidify their occupation of Poland. This apparently includes imprisoning any Poles whose educated background makes them potentially useful to Polish resistance groups.[11]

Quickly it reaches the point where the Germans regularly round up Jews in the same violent manner—not simply through notification but by picking people up off the streets, randomly and relentlessly. The situation to which we have now become accustomed is quite surreal: at any given moment, the chaotic roundups can begin. People try to hide in their homes or elsewhere. But once the roundups are completed a few hours later, we then travel freely about town. It is as if little at all has happened.

However, knowing that just walking down the street at the wrong time can lead to forced labor, we stop venturing outside our house unless it is necessary. I am now spending most days helping my father in the tannery, carrying the heavy pails of water on my shoulders from the well. Not only does this hard labor cause my shoulders to develop blisters, but it also leaves me exposed to danger.

Usually I try to walk between home and work with Berale, who is one of my closest friends. His father sells horses next to our tannery. Before the war Berale and I had been schoolmates. He had always been an excellent student and a great athlete. After school we had often played soccer together. And when it was warm, we had gone for picnics on Saturday with our groups of friends. But now we are concerned, first and foremost, with being safe. We figure that by sticking together during our walks, we'll be better able to spot trouble.

One day as Berale and I are walking home together, we see three uniformed Germans descending toward us from their headquarters up the hill. There aren't any other streets for us to turn onto at that part of the road, so we quickly agree to continue walking down the road. But I have a feeling of dread that I am sure Berale shares. I feel my heart beating faster and faster. When we get to within a few yards of the soldiers on the road, they stop walking. We try to walk casually past them, but they step in front of us and block our path. Now knowing that something is very wrong, I say to Berale, "Quick, you go this way. I go that way." I dart around them, and Berale too runs away from them.

Without pausing to look back, I turn a few corners and then hide in some bushes. I can hear the sound of my own breathing. I try to be calm and breathe as quietly as possible. After about thirty minutes I can no longer hear the soldiers, so I step out of the bushes as quietly as I can and run down a back alley to my house. Not wanting to worry anyone, I don't tell anyone about what has happened. But I go to bed that night praying fervently that Berale has eluded the soldiers.

In the morning, Berale's father comes to our house and informs us that my friend had not returned home yesterday. I tell him what had happened. Several days go by and Berale still has not returned. I know they must have caught him. Everyone's worst fears are confirmed a few days later by a man named Stefan, who works near the soldiers' barracks. He tells Berale's father that he had seen Berale brought to the barracks and that he believes Berale was sexually assaulted and killed.

I try not to think about how Berale must have died. But I can't stop wishing that I had done something differently that could have saved his life. I also know that if I had run in the same direction as Berale, I probably would have died along with my friend. Only luck had saved me.

With the frequency and brutality of roundups now increasing, in the middle of 1940 my father decides to build a hiding place for us. With Symcha's help we build a double wall in my father's tannery. The hiding place saves us from the roundups almost daily.

Several thousand more Jews arrive from western Poland between the spring of 1940 and the spring of 1941. Our small town can barely handle the influx. Even with each small Jewish home in town now sheltering two to three families, hundreds of the newcomers are forced to live in the synagogue. Meeting life's daily needs becomes increasingly difficult. Food is scarce. Because of the German authorities' strict rationing of food, we have barely any meat. And because the Germans threaten to imprison or kill any Jews who engage in ritual slaughter, we have even less kasher meat. It must be both slaughtered and obtained secretly. Thus there is simply not enough of it to feed all the many religiously observant Jews in our town.

Of course, everyone knows that according to *halachah*, certain Jewish customs can be adjusted if necessary to save a person's life.[12] But no one feels comfortable eating foods that have been forbidden to us for centuries and that have certainly never touched our palates before. When it becomes evident what a serious problem this dilemma is creating—both physically and spiritually—for the town's many observant Jews, my father tells us that he has decided to bribe a policeman into giving us a cow for ritual slaughter. He reminds us that the entire process must remain secret.

My father arranges for a *shochet* to slaughter the cow in the barn by our house in the middle of the night.[13] That same night the meat dealers also come and pick up the meat for distribution. As I hear the men tiptoeing past our house in the dead of night, I think about how my father is risking his life—and all our lives—just to have kasher meat. My father could have told everyone that it was too dangerous to covertly slaughter the cow and then the people would have been forced to eat the non-kasher meat. But my father, I think, must have had good reason to take this risk. I admire his courage and am proud to have him as my father.

When I awake the next morning, I find a pit in our backyard filled with the blood of the cow. The hole is about two feet deep and four feet in diameter. Cows have a lot of blood! And because of the laws of kasher slaughter, it had been necessary to drain as much of the blood as possible from the cow. But this has created another major problem for us: if anyone finds this pool of blood, he or she will immediately know that an animal has been illegally slaughtered. My father's courage now seems more like recklessness. But he quickly arrives at a solution: he instructs Brancha and me to quietly take pail after pail of blood and innards away to the hills near the house and mix the blood into the sand and dirt. I have never done any work like this before. At first the sight and smell of the thick blood repulses me. But I persist, knowing that this work needs to be done for my family to survive. We *schlepp* the blood throughout the morning until all signs of the slaughter are erased.[14]

With so many men being taken away to work, people have little or no money for food. Sima's family, which had been poor before the war began, becomes more and more desperate for necessities like food. She has three brothers and sisters, plus her parents. Aware of how they are struggling, my father begins giving me food and money to deliver to them whenever I can. He also pays me for helping out in the tannery, and I start giving some of this money to Sima's family as well. Her parents are extremely grateful. Whenever I arrive at their house, they hug me and tell me that I am part of their family. And after receiving any gifts from me, her father always blesses me and tells me that I will be remembered for my good deeds for them and others.

On June 22, 1941, Germany attacks the Soviet Union. This permanently closes off the possibility of any more Jews escaping across the Bug River, which is now a war front. Within days of the attacks, many of the few Jews who had already escaped to the Soviet Union return to Izbica to avoid dying in the latest German offensive. Jakub, however, does not return. We still have no idea where he is or whether he is even still alive.

During the fall of 1941, my father hears that the Germans have asked the Judenrat to provide several Jewish men who can guard arms depots in the nearby woods. With so many troops being diverted to the eastern front, perhaps the Germans are short of men. Judging this job to be preferable to hard labor in a work camp, my father suggests that I volunteer for the assignment. I follow his advice.

At nightfall I am taken along with several other boys to the forest about one mile outside Izbica to relieve the boys who have already spent the day shift manning a guard station in front of the depot. We are instructed that if we hear anything out of the ordinary, such as Polish underground fighters trying to sabotage or steal the munitions, we should radio the Germans for help. That night, as we huddle around a fire that we feed frequently with wood to fend off the cold, we discuss what we would really do if anyone approached. We all sympathize with the resistance fighters and agree that we would never alert the Germans to their whereabouts. Rather than radio the Germans, we would try to identify ourselves to any fighters, offer whatever assistance we can, and wait until the fighters have enough time to get away before we would tell the Germans that we had been ambushed. But we also fear for our safety because we know these guerillas can strike without warning and kill us instantly. Fortunately, we are never tested.

Two weeks of guard duty elapse quickly, without incident. Then we are told that our services are no longer needed.

Soon after our work assignment ends, a Gestapo squad commander arrives in Izbica.[15] His name is SS Unterscharführer Kurt Engels, and he is assisted by SS Rottenführer Ludwig Klemm, who is a Volksdeutscher.[16] Together the two men quickly set up an office just a few blocks from our house in the small white building that had formerly been the Polish police headquarters. We all know what this means. No longer will Izbica be governed by regular units of the German armed forces; now we will be subject to the direct control of Hitler's elite SS, a cadre infamous for brutalizing civilians.

Except for their uniforms, Engels and Klemm appear at first glance to be ordinary Germans—tall, handsome, and professional. But one of their first actions is to arrest any of Izbica's remaining non-Jewish intellectuals, such as professors, teachers, and priests. They are all taken to the prison across the street from the police headquarters. There, according to what Symcha hears from Izbica's main physician, Dr. Marienstras, some of them are shot, and the others are sent to Lublin. Dr. Marienstras says that he was forced by Engels to sign death certificates falsely stating that the murdered had died of natural causes.

Things quickly get even worse. Engels's depravity becomes further evident when one day he walks out of his office and, without any warning, calmly shoots a few Jews who are walking past the building. This atrocity turns out to be more than a one-time occurrence. My friend Josele falls victim to Engels a few days later. One quiet morning he is shot and killed as he walks past the police headquarters. I can hear Josele's mother crying in the street from several blocks away.

Engels soon finds yet another way to kill. Over the following weeks, he and Klemm develop a bloody habit: every few days they travel around town, either by foot or motorcycle, on a shooting rampage, randomly murdering a few people as they sleep in their beds or walk down the street. We all flee and hide wherever is closest—in our secret hiding places, under beds, anywhere. I am almost shot on several occasions, but the closest call comes one day when I am walking down the street and see them approaching. I quickly dive behind a well and hold my breath. I am not very well concealed. Miraculously, they walk past without seeing me. Had they noticed me, I have no doubt they would have shot me in cold blood.

We decide to build several new hiding places. We dig a hole that begins inside our house and leads to a pit on the other side of the wall of the house. We also build a subterranean hideout beneath the living room. The main difference between the two hiding places is that the one inside the house is bigger (because its interior location has made it easier to secretly excavate) and the one outside is better concealed (accessed via a sliding wall that we have built into the side of our house, as opposed to the double door that leads to the indoor hiding place). We agree that if a roundup starts, we will all go into the hiding places for the entire night. Despite being huddled together, we will probably be cold. There will also be little air to breathe, even though we have installed tiny tubes to bring air into the pits.

We even build a third hiding place in our attic. It consists of a double door covered by straw that we buy from a farmer. But it is not nearly as well concealed as our other two hideouts. We agree to use it only as a last resort for ourselves or to hide any visitors or additional occupants of the house who can't fit into the other hiding places.

But there are still new decrees that we can't hide from. Though it is the middle of a cold winter, one day Schultz goes house to house with a few German soldiers demanding that we turn over every fur coat for use on the eastern front. He knows that my father owns one of the nicest fur coats in the city—Symcha had bought it for my father in Warsaw—so we have no choice but to hand it over.

One night Symcha returns home from work with a harrowing story. He says that he had needed to travel to Krasnystaw earlier in the day to procure medications for a makeshift hospital that necessity had forced us to erect in the synagogue. Dr. Marienstras had given Symcha a statement saying that Symcha is a representative of the hospital and specifying exactly how much of each medication he is authorized to pick up. Symcha had taken the train to Krasnystaw and picked up the medications from the Germans' district office there. All went smoothly until Symcha had begun walking back to the railroad station. He had been stopped by a German soldier and asked to show what he was carrying. Symcha had explained that he was delivering medical supplies and displayed his letter of authorization as well as the supplies. But when the soldier saw that the supplies included a container of rubbing alcohol, he had accused Symcha of smuggling alcohol. Symcha had protested his innocence, but there had been little else he could do. The soldier had placed all the supplies to the side, and then took Symcha to the outskirts of the town, where a German guard was stationed at an outpost. The soldier had informed the guard that Symcha was a smuggler. The guard had taken hold of his gun and told Symcha to run. Symcha had figured out what this meant: he was about to be used for target practice. Not willing to be killed so easily, however, Symcha had pretended not to understand the order. Then he had heard the soldier say to the guard, "Hurry, the commanding officer is approaching." Symcha had seized the opportunity. He had begun yelling and running in the direction of the approaching officer, hoping that the guard would not risk launching a stray bullet in the direction of the officer. The gambit had paid off. No shots were fired. When Symcha reached the officer, he had shown him his papers and explained what had happened. The officer had sent the guard back to his post and personally escorted Symcha to the train station, where his supplies were waiting.

The spring of 1942 brings warmer weather, but otherwise no relief from the daily terror. One evening I am walking home with my cousin Alter. He is blond, blue-eyed, and a gifted athlete. Before the war we had always swum together in the Wiepsz River, which flows along the outer limits of town. Alter was such an excellent swimmer that we all had thought he would win medals if he swam competitively. But he could only dream of such glory. We had no swim team in Izbica, and now that we are at war, Alter no longer has any chance of swimming in competitions in Warsaw. Alter and I have just completed our private tutoring session with a teacher named Jankiel. In the middle of our short walk, we sense the beginning of a commotion. Looking around, we see that Germans and strange soldiers dressed in black uniforms have surrounded the town and descended upon it from all sides. Aided by Schultz and a few other local collaborators, the black-uniformed soldiers—who seem to be speaking to each other in Ukrainian—are going house to house along with the Germans, rounding up Jews.[17]

We climb to the roof of a neighbor's home. We then cover ourselves with a few bundles of straw that we find there and leave spaces for air. Through the straw we watch as the squad continues its roundup from house to house, tearing dozens of Jews from their homes. Most of these unfortunate victims are the non-natives of Izbica who know of no good places to hide. We wait on the rooftop for several hours until the sounds coming from town subside, and it finally seems safe to come down. We carefully make it back to our homes, which are next to each other, by cutting behind as many homes as we can.

At my house I find everyone except Rywka and her son. My mother is greatly worried. She says that Rywka had been in town with Josele doing errands when the roundups began, and they have not returned to the hiding place. Alter reports that his older brother, Ichak, has also gone missing. We know that all the persons we cannot account for have very likely been caught in the roundup.

As we walk throughout town the following day, searching in vain for Rywka, Josele, and Ichak, the horror of what has occurred quickly becomes evident: about half the population, or several thousand Jews, has simply vanished. Among them are Sima and her entire family. They had probably been in their house when the akcja began.

From my father's friends in the Judenrat, we learn that the Germans had ordered them to provide the names of several thousand people to be taken. The Judenrat had no choice but to obey; failure to comply would have meant that the entire town would be taken. After everyone seized in the roundup had been herded to the train station, the Judenrat had informed them that they would be resettled. The people had been given bread for the journey, but we still fear the worst.

Because in the past Symcha had taught his dance classes at the Officers' Club, he is on good terms with a member of the Polish police. Symcha asks his contact about the whereabouts of the people who have been taken away. The policeman's answer is that the train had gone to the town of Bełżec.

In the next few days, rumors quickly spread about Bełżec: similar transports of thousands of Jews from other towns and cities have been arriving almost daily at a camp in Bełżec; so many thousands of people cannot possibly fit in one camp; and ominously, the stench of decomposing bodies pervades the nearby areas.

Though we do not sit *shivah* for her, we know that Rywka, as well as my nephew, my cousin, and Sima and her family, are probably all dead.[18] Rywka is the only one of my siblings to have children. I remember the day she had first given birth. It had been a difficult delivery, and we had all stayed in the adjoining room praying and crying until little Josele arrived. Now both she and Josele are gone, and we are left to care for Rywka's remaining daughter.

It is the first time that I have experienced the death of someone so close to me. I hope that our large family will be able to depend on one another for support during this period of terrible sadness. Surely we will grieve and eventually come to terms with our loss, just as everyone had apparently done following Chaim's tragic accident as well as after the peaceful deaths of my grandparents before I was born. But this seems different. Never have so many loved ones been torn from us at once. And never have they been murdered. Everyone's grief is like none I could have ever imagined. And I am all the more shaken by the loss of my beloved Sima.

With no end to the German occupation in sight, I now fear even more for my own life and the lives of everyone around me. I worry about further tragedies. I wonder who will be next to disappear or die.

My father is forced to close his tannery because there is a shortage of raw materials. But the Germans still need the town's leather factory, so it remains open. The factory's Jewish owners, Mr. Altman and Mr. Blanc, decide that they can use my father's skills there. So he begins working as a supervisor at the factory. This means we can no longer rely on the hiding place in the tannery. But my father tells us that the leather factory will be one of the safest places to be during any future roundups. After all, its employees are needed for the German war effort. And because he now works there, he can ensure that all our names are listed on the employee roles. If a roundup ever occurs, he says, then my sisters, my mother, my niece, and I should go immediately to the leather factory. There we can pose as factory employees. Both Mr. Altman and Mr. Blanc have also told their family members to do exactly the same thing. Symcha will be safest in the hospital, and we can still hide in the house if, for some reason, we cannot make it to the leather factory in time.

Just a few weeks later, our worst fears are realized: another violent *akcja* and deportation occurs. According to plan my mother, two sisters, niece, and I run to the factory as soon as the roundups begin. There we join a group of people whose relatives are also working there. Together we nervously wait for the akcja to end.

Within minutes several policemen enter the factory. They order everyone out of the building. Despite our protests that we are working for the Germans, we are forced out of the factory and marched to the train station, where cattle cars await. They begin pushing us into the cattle cars, when finally one of our group—a member of either the Altman or the Blanc family—is able to provide a German officer with a document stating that we are producing leather for the Germans. The officer orders a halt to the loading process. Then the officer calls out the names of the families: Altman, Białowicz, Blanc, and several more. We step forward and are separated from the desperate people waiting to be transported. All the workers and their families are spared in this way.

A few minutes later, the cattle cars pull away. Their human cargo numbers in the hundreds, including every member of the family from Warsaw who had been living with us, as well as Uncle Ichak and Aunt Chana. My father is told by the Judenrat that they have been taken away for "resettlement." We continue to wonder if it will be really possible to avoid their fate.

But over the next few days, something strange occurs: the Germans decorate the town with beautiful and abundant displays of flowers in front of every house. What are they planning? Most people speculate that a German dignitary is about to visit. But the next visitors to our town are several trainloads of Jews from Germany and Czechoslovakia. The German authorities tell them they are being resettled in Izbica. Apparently, the recent beautification of our town has been undertaken to make the newcomers feel comfortable.[19]

Entire families arrive in passenger cars, with all their luggage and belongings. Some of them are highly cultured. They truly believe that they are being resettled, despite the cruelties they have already experienced. After all, a few of the newcomers are decorated war veterans who fought for the German and the Austro-Hungarian empires during the First World War; these older German Jewish and Austrian Jewish gentlemen now wear their medals publicly, as if to remind their oppressors of the thanks owed them. But I doubt whether even their status as military heroes can protect them from the likes of Engels, Klemm, and the squads conducting the roundups. After all, they are still Jews. As I watch the German authorities carry out what I know is probably just an evil deception, I feel sad and powerless to help these thousands of foreigners.

The Judenrat is asked to provide accommodations for all the incoming families. There are not nearly enough vacant homes to do this, but the Judenrat does what it can. Some of the families are sheltered, usually two or three to a house, in the homes that have been deserted by families previously taken to Bełżec. Other arriving families are sent by the Judenrat to stay with families that have enough space to host them. And that is how we meet the Rosenbergers.

3 |

The Rosenbergers

Our newest houseguests turn out to be a wealthy Jewish family, very prominent in their native Germany. Before the war, the head of the family, Emil Rosenberger, had owned a large shop in the Black Forest city of Karlsruhe, selling iron products. He is to live with us, along with his wife, Erna, and their two daughters, Ilse and Herta.

Famous rabbis have stayed with us before, but this is different. This causes a small-scale sensation. My mother has to shoo neighbors away from our doors to keep them from staring. Friends tease me, "So, Fiszel, what's it like living with royalty?"

In truth it isn't at all enviable. Their celebrity sets everyone on edge. It is difficult not to offer them the best of everything, including our own portions of what little food there is. Only through conscious effort can we ever bridge our differences with the Rosenbergers. It would have been impossible to throw together two more different families. Everything we are, they are not. Where the Rosenbergers are progressive and assimilated, my family is religious. Where Emil sells modern iron products, my father produces leather. Where Mrs. Rosenberger visits museums and hosts aristocrats, my mother bakes matze and reads prayers to the illiterate.

Both Mr. and Mrs. Rosenberger at least make the pretense of being polite. But they still appear too absorbed in their own personal worries to notice the feelings or efforts of anyone else. It must be difficult for them to digest the indignity of living with us. With the concurrent arrival of a new guest family from Warsaw—consisting of my Aunt Cira, her husband, and their two sons, Fiszel and Chaim—our quarters become certainly far more cramped than any living situation that the Rosenbergers have ever experienced. The attic is occupied by Fiszel, who is in his twenties and suffers from lung disease, along with Chaim, who is in his early thirties and had taught engineering classes in Warsaw. Meanwhile, Aunt Cira and my uncle—who are both tailors—share Rywka's old room with little Sara. The Rosenbergers are forced to sleep on straw mattresses on our living room floor. My family has always shared beds—I sleep next to my father—and have lived with many people in the house before (though certainly not this many), so we are at least a little more accustomed to the crowded accommodations than are our aristocratic guests.

The two Rosenberger daughters retain some of the airs of their parents but not their personal distance. Ilse is a sweet but quiet eighteen-year-old girl. She gets on well with Toba, who, unlike most young girls in Izbica, has tasted life outside town. I tend to speak more with seventeen-year-old Herta. At first I am nervous talking with her—not only is she a year older than me, but she is strikingly beautiful as well. But Herta manages to maintain a lightness and a sense of humor that sets me at ease. We have fun trying to bridge the language divide between her German and my Yiddish.[1] When she informs me that she finds my accent "cute," I allow myself to wonder whether she could possibly share the feelings that I am beginning to have for her.

As it turns out, the Rosenbergers have a hidden cache of jewels brought with them from Germany. When we explain to Mr. Rosenberger how certain necessities can be purchased, he gives me a ruby to sell on the black market, making sure to tell me what it was worth when he had first purchased it for his wife.

I return home a few hours later, having sold the ruby for one-twentieth of what Mr. Rosenberger had paid for it in Germany. I am surprised to find that this does not bother him. He simply shrugs, smiles, and thanks me. Apparently he has a heart. With the tip that he gives me, he tells me to go buy some ice cream. He then hands all the remaining money to my mother and suggests that she use it to buy food for the Sabbath.

When we finally sit down for our first Sabbath meal, I am eager to see how these German Jews will participate in this joyful weekly ritual. Are they really that different? In what they wear, they certainly are. They arrive at the table dressed much more formally than us; we are not wealthy enough to have such clothing. I have one very basic suit that Symcha had brought from Warsaw when I became *bar mitzvah* more than three years ago.[2] We have already altered the suit several times since then to accommodate my growth spurt. Though it still fits me well, I can't help but feel inadequate in the presence of Mr. Rosenberger and his much finer attire.

The Rosenbergers have lost almost everything—their home, most of their possessions, their high social and economic status—but they seem to at least find some comfort in the traditional Jewish customs. Because they come from the more assimilated Reformed Jewish tradition, they mostly just observe as my father leads everyone in reciting every word of the traditional prayers, entirely in the Hebrew language. But Herta, whom I make sure to sit next to, continually asks questions throughout the ritual. I like her inquisitive nature. I kid with her: "You should have been here a few weeks ago to help me ask the Four Questions at the Passover *seder!*"[3]

The shared experience of the Sabbath draws our two families closer together. Moreover, because of the state of things, we cannot treat the Rosenbergers as honored guests for too long anyway. Everyone understands that we need to overcome many challenges with whatever we have, and we have no choice but to do it together. These difficult times force the Rosenbergers' true natures to be revealed. Slowly, reluctantly, they become people.

Despite all our differences—and there are still many that remain—we are beginning to act like one family rather than two. Our home is becoming theirs. You can even hear it in the way we bicker—not at all out of resentment, but out of comfort with one another and our need to feel like normal human beings again. Argument for the sake of argument is a luxury, and we recognize it. Our fathers in particular enjoy respectful but lively ongoing debates with each other. "What do you think the Germans intend to do with all of us Jews?" asks my father during dinner one night.

"The authorities told us that we are being permanently resettled in the East," Mr. Rosenberger asserts. "As long as we continue to perform the work they assign to us, I have little reason to doubt that they will achieve their goals. They always do."

"I hope you're right," my father responds. He certainly does not share Mr. Rosenberger's faith—or is it hope?—in Hitler's government, nor do I. But we keep our fears to ourselves. We expect that eventually the Germans will attempt to send the Rosenbergers—and us too—to Bełżec like so many others before us.

But a month passes, then two months, and the Rosenbergers appear to be one of the few families remaining out of those who have arrived in April. It all seems strange, but my father refuses to speculate about the reasons. When I ask him why he thinks the Rosenbergers have been spared, he only says, "One does not challenge a miracle."

However, my father must have his theories, as do I. Mr. Rosenberger has been in contact with several members of the Judenrat—since his arrival, some non-Polish Jews have been appointed to the council—but has refused membership himself. Perhaps it is his influence with these privileged officials that explains the placement of his family in our relatively comfortable home. The work details he is assigned to by the Judenrat are also among the least difficult.

Our two families have by now developed a symbiotic relationship. We rely on them for the finances necessary for survival, and they rely on us for the knowledge and expertise required to navigate life in Izbica. Mr. Rosenberger trusts me—"You are like a member of our family," he likes to tell me—and demonstrates his confidence by continuing to send me on important errands. I conduct all the sales of his jewels and make all his purchases with the money gained from them. When the jewels run out, he gives me watches to sell with exotic names like Eterna, IWC, and Patek Phillipe. But he always shares the proceeds evenly; as his family receives, so do we. And after a successful sale, he often buys ice cream for me. But I always prefer when he tips me with money because it allows me to buy chocolates and flowers for Herta.

With each passing day, my feelings for Herta are growing. She is as beautiful as she is bright. Her hair is long, brown, and curly. Her face is roundish, like an owl's, with soft brown eyes just as wide. One day Herta notices me gazing intently at her while she is writing in her diary. Misinterpreting, she asks me to apologize for not respecting her privacy.

"Why should I apologize for simply staring at someone so beautiful?" I boldly answer.

She smiles and returns to her writing. It's the closest I have come so far to revealing my true feelings to Herta. And she has not responded badly. In fact, I see her distinctly blushing as she continues writing. I wonder how the war could have brought something so wonderful into my life. And I look forward to the moment when I might be able to kiss her. I don't know when it will arrive, but when it does I will be the happiest boy in Izbica.

The next day, as I am making a transaction for Mr. Rosenberger, a roundup begins. I run to the nearest hiding place that I know of: the leather factory. There I find about forty other Jews crammed into the two large pits where leather had been processed underground. I join them while several factory workers frantically attempt to conceal the pit with wood and barrels. But a few local collaborators apparently know about this hole, and they lead the Germans to it. We have no choice but to surrender. We are marched through the middle of town on the way to the train station. As everyone marches, a few Christian townspeople stand watching from the side.

I know I will die if I don't do something to save myself. I want so much to live: for me, for my family, and now for Herta. I have to do something. As I walk between a few taller adults, I quickly remove my Star of David armband and place it in my pocket. Then I inch to the side and slip out of the line of doomed people. I walk in the opposite direction, as casually as possible. Somehow, amid the commotion, no one notices me or denounces me to the Germans. When I come home, everyone—including, to my great delight, Herta—showers me with hugs and kisses. Symcha tells me that his friend on the police force has told him everyone was sent to Bełżec.

But I am so preoccupied with Herta that the dreadful news affects me less than it would have otherwise.

4

Fritz

One June afternoon I am home alone studying when I hear the sound of a car approaching. I put my book down and look out the window. There, just down the street, is a Mercedes. The car stops. Out comes the driver, an officer dressed in a gray uniform. His collar bears the unmistakable insignia of the SS. He checks a slip of paper and walks toward our home, our door.

My heart sinks.

Few things are certain. One never knows what might be taken from him next, where one might be sent, if tomorrow your home will be yours. But one thing is near certain: if an officer of the SS comes to your home, your life is at an end. His presence means death. My only comfort is that I am at home alone. At least the others still have a chance to live.

I duck under a bed, hidden by the darkness. The SS officer leans his head in, searching. Then he enters the house through the front door. I catch a clear glimpse of him now. Standing straight, he is tall, very broad, with a dark, sad face. This, I think to myself, must be the face of the *malach hamavet.*[1]

He closes the door and approaches the windows, then lowers the curtains, darkening the room. He is young but supremely composed. Surely these are the methodical preparations of a trained murderer.

A thousand thoughts course through my mind: Who is he here to kill? My father? Mr. Rosenberger? Maybe I am already an orphan. I wonder if I should recite the *Shema* in preparation for my death.[2]

If he takes a few more steps, he will probably see me under the bed. I hold my breath so as not to gasp.

I then hear voices approaching from the back of the house. They are returning: Mrs. Rosenberger, with Ilse and Herta. And they don't know what awaits them in our home.

They are seconds away from entering the room where the SS man stands. I want so badly to warn them. But to utter the slightest sound would surely bring about my own immediate end. And if they could run, they would not make it far before getting caught in this land that is still so foreign to them. I curse myself for not having a gun, let alone never having learned to shoot one.

They draw closer to the house's rear door. Within moments their fate will be sealed. Maybe the SS man will kill them before my very eyes. I have never felt so completely helpless. I shut my eyes so as not to see their lives taken in front of me.

They enter the room. But instead of orders, shouts, or shots, I hear something much different: polite greetings, laughing, and hugging. Mrs. Rosenberger offers coffee to the officer and begins heating water. I can't understand what I am seeing. Why has the SS officer not killed them? Could Mr. Rosenberger be bribing the SS to treat his family well? Or worse, are the Rosenbergers collaborating with the Germans?

They talk as if they were old friends. The Rosenbergers refer to this man not by his title but by his first name, Fritz. With my limited ability to understand the German language, I can make out that they inquire into the whereabouts of family and friends in Germany. Fritz does not know much. The officer shares news of the work he has been doing at a nearby base. The Rosenbergers describe the goings-on in Izbica. They ask if he can do anything to tame Engels and Klemm. He says he is "helpless against those madmen."

The officer departs, promising to return soon. But without knowing if I can trust the Rosenbergers anymore, I don't want to reveal myself. Given Mr. Rosenberger's privileged position in German society, it seems conceivable that he could be spying for the Germans. Whatever he is involved with, however, I am sure that Herta will tell me the truth. I decide to wait until I can confront her in private about my discovery.

As soon as everyone leaves the room, I sneak out of the house. After circling the block, I return home and immediately ask Herta to go on a walk with me. There is a small wooded area between the rear of our house and the cemetery. Here we can talk to each other privately. As we stroll among the trees, I reveal to her that I saw everything. Fritz. The warm greetings. The cordial embraces. The friendly conversation. I tell Herta that I had feared she would be killed. She is shocked. But she refuses to tell me what is going on. "My father ordered me not to tell anyone," she says. "It is a secret I cannot reveal even to you."

I cannot believe that she will not explain it to me. I am not just curious but also hurt by her secrecy. "I thought we trusted each other," I say.

"Fiszel, of course I trust you. But sometimes it is better not to know certain things. We could all be killed."

I have no choice but to accept her answer.

Over the next two weeks, we continue spending all our free time with each other. But I begin to feel more distant from Herta. Each day my theory about her father's covert activities on behalf of the Germans becomes increasingly plausible in my own mind. Given that Mr. Rosenberger might have served in the German Army during the First World War, perhaps his allegiances still lie with his country. Furthermore, surely many of Germany's elite businessmen—and perhaps even a few complicit Jews—have connections within the Nazi Party.

I trust Herta, but can she be unwittingly aiding her father's spy mission? So many doubts race through my mind. And it affects our relationship. I grow increasingly less talkative when we are together. Herta picks up on it quickly. "What's wrong?" she asks.

"I can't stop thinking about the German officer. It was like you were all such good friends with him."

"I'm sorry. I just can't tell you. My father forbade me."

Then, a few days later, it happens again. The same officer arrives. I hide, only to witness the same hugging and kissing between Herta's family and the mysterious German.

After everyone is gone, I again take her aside.

As we begin walking, I try to convince her to reveal her secret. "You owe me an explanation," I say. "This can't go on like this."

"But my father said that the secret must remain within our family. Nobody else can know."

"But didn't your father also say that I am like a member of your family?"

She thinks for a few moments. "Come, sit down with me," she says.

We sit beneath a few tall and shady trees. Finally, Herta proceeds to explain everything.

"The officer is a member of our family," she says. "He is a distant cousin. He is Jewish. Because his side of the family intermarried several generations ago, the Germans did not consider him to be Jewish. But he always considered himself Jewish and so did we. He joined the SS only to try using his influence to save as many of his relatives as possible."

I ask her what this cousin, Fritz, is doing in this area. She tells me he is a lieutenant with responsibilities in our district. Had it not been for him, she says, she and her family might be dead by now. Fritz has arranged for her father to be assigned to specialized engineering details that have shielded him from transports to the camps. Fritz has pulled strings to spare them at every step, keeping them alive and as comfortable as possible. Though Fritz and her father refuse to talk about it, Herta believes that Fritz may have interceded to help free her father from the Dachau concentration camp in 1938. During Mr. Rosenberger's one-month imprisonment in Dachau, however, Herta and her sister both paid a dear price: they sacrificed their valuable positions on a list of Jewish children eligible for emigration to the United Kingdom because they had not wanted to leave their mother alone. Once their father returned, they had decided to stay together as a family because they hoped Fritz would have the power to save them. But he had been unable to prevent their deportation to Izbica.[3]

I can scarcely believe what I am hearing. Then Herta shows me a photograph of her family arm in arm with a younger version of Fritz. Not too old a photo, although the paper is worn and wrinkled. His face looks so much softer in the photo than in real life, so much more capable of feeling. She tells me how she has kept the picture with her, always, sewn into the inside of her pocket.

"But how can this possibly be right?" I ask. "How does one justify such direct collaboration with Hitler?"

"Because of him we were able to avoid deportation from Germany for much longer than we might have," Herta replies.

"And what good is that luxury now?"

"It brought me here, didn't it? To you . . ."

This is the first time she has admitted to having feelings for me. I feel my head go light. She kisses me on the cheek, her lips just touching the corner of my mouth. Her hand grasps mine and does not let go. We begin to walk. I am elated.

Herta opens up to me as we stroll beneath the trees. She reveals how afraid she is and how she feels sorry for her parents, whom she knows are just putting on brave faces. She tells me how important my support has been to her over the past few tumultuous months.

I feel much the same way as Herta. I confess my affections, to their fullest extent. To my wonder she is not put off by them, or me, in the slightest. We eagerly conspire how to best inform her father of her interest in a commoner and worse, a religious commoner. But we agree not to reveal our secret just yet.

Despite my immediate excitement over this new stage in our relationship, I find it difficult to erase from my thoughts the image of a man in an SS uniform hugging Herta. After all, Fritz must have done terrible things in order to obtain and keep his post. Yet his intentions are meant to be benevolent. The line between right and wrong seems disturbingly blurry.

Ever perceptive, Herta immediately senses my distraction. After a long silence, she says, "He's never killed anyone, Jewish or not. I know this."

But from the way she says this I know that she speaks not from knowledge but from her heart. A wish. Blind faith.

I learn that Fritz is not stationed in Izbica, where Engels reigns, but in Lublin. There he works in the district's main SS office. This gives him power and access. As it turns out, it gives him chocolate as well. When Herta and I return from the woods, we find that Fritz has left behind a package full of sweets. Mr. Rosenberger hands me several pounds of chocolates and asks me to trade them for as much food as possible. I don't ask about how he procured the chocolate, nor does Mr. Rosenberger volunteer the information to any of us.

We all eat well that night, as chocolate trades quite highly in Izbica. And a square remains for each of us for dessert. My family does not eat the chocolate until the next day, however, for we observe the law of kashrus dictating that we wait six hours before consuming dairy products after having eaten meat. This does not spoil the good mood that evening, though. As the Rosenbergers enjoy their chocolates, Mrs. Rosenberger teases my father that he should have eaten his chocolate before dinner. We all enjoy a laugh.

Over the following weeks, I still cannot help but dwell on Fritz and what he has done, what he is doing. I constantly ask Herta for details about him. And though she keeps none of her own secrets from me, of her mysterious cousin she will tell me precious little. I learn that his chief duty is organizing battle supplies for the German battalions. To me this seems yet another inexcusable act of complicity, and I again confront Herta with my misgivings about her cousin. Herta responds with another explanation of Fritz's service to the German Reich. She says that the Nazi Party knows that he has a Jewish ancestor and this puts him in danger. Right now, she explains, German citizens with at least one Jewish grandparent are being treated as Jews in Germany. This does not include Fritz, but this provision of the law, she says, can also change at any moment. By serving his country faithfully, she says, Fritz hopes to prove his loyalty to Germany. "But," I ask, "did he need to go the length of joining the SS to prove his loyalty?" This, Herta reiterates, has afforded him greater power to save their family. "But," I insist, "what about the other families?"

I begin to see Fritz in my nightmares. I imagine all the terrible things he has done to maintain his secret identity. Herta's assurance that he has not taken a life seems increasingly naive, hopeful. No, I think, surely he has been tested. And even if he has somehow managed to avoid killing anyone, he has certainly been compelled to join his comrades in the daily humiliation and mistreatment of Jews. Has he simply watched when others beat Jewish men and cut their beards, or has he participated in order to avoid the suspicion of his peers?

Fritz continues to steal in for visits every so often, always unannounced, making his visits all the more disconcerting. With him nearby I am like a child in my fears. Does he still say his Jewish prayers? Even if he only recites the prayers without vocalizing them, does he dare to pray while in uniform? I can't help but believe him supernatural. Part Aryan and part Jewish. Surely a being with two hearts and minds has powers beyond that of a normal man. This man Fritz goes against everything that has become our reality. He is like a ghost to me, an apparition. He is an impossibility, and yet he is real.

And I cannot even discuss Fritz with Symcha, my brother and most trusted friend. But I do reveal to him my secret romance with Herta. He, in turn, tells me of his new girlfriend: a beautiful girl named Golda from the town of Koło whom he has been courting ever since her arrival in Izbica.

5

Summer 1942

The summer goes by mercifully with only a few transports. But we still live in constant fear of Engels and Klemm, whose outbursts continue to take many lives. One day they gun down Uncle Szlome's two beautiful blonde daughters, Sara and Rachel, who are only nineteen and twenty-two. Alter witnesses the murders from his window. His sisters die in his arms. Now he has lost not just his parents but all three of his siblings.

Alter is inconsolable. For days on end he walks around in tears. When he talks, nobody can understand what he is saying. It is as if he has become a different person. I worry that my once-strong cousin is now mentally ill. We all try to help him. We comfort him in our home and feed him every day. Our neighbors try to talk to him, but they can't help. I take him out for a walk and try to convince him to look at the bright side. I tell him, "Alter, we are young, we are going to survive, and we are going to take vengeance." When that doesn't work, I say, "It is an act of God. What can we do? God will take care of the Nazis eventually. They will be defeated and destroyed like they destroyed our brothers and sisters. The destruction is already taking place. The Allies are already taking vengeance for us, bombing the Germans from all sides."

But nothing any of us say or do can help Alter. And I can't blame him. When my own sister and Sima were taken away to the camps, it had been very difficult, but at least I had not seen them being murdered. Alter, on the other hand, had beheld everything. If my eyes had seen what his had, I would have gone through the same or maybe worse emotions than he. I probably would have committed suicide.

Finally, Symcha tells us that he has found a psychiatrist among the German Jews who says he can help. The psychiatrist treats Alter with a medication that seems to calm him. The fits of crying abate, but now Alter stops talking almost completely. I fear that my cousin will never recover fully. We all watch over him to make sure he doesn't relapse. Everyone in the family feels responsible for Alter, and we make sure that he continues dining with us at every meal. He becomes like a younger brother to me.

With Symcha's encouragement, my feelings for Herta are growing. Though I still silently fear that either or both of us will be murdered or taken away by the Germans at any moment, this does not stop me from drawing closer and closer to her. In fact, our precarious situation is pushing us together. She is my one solace from the world, and I hers. Since our feelings are still a secret and privacy is so infrequent, I often express myself in writing: short letters left by her bedside, under her books. I find I have a knack for Yiddish poetry. Our affections have blossomed into love.

Whenever possible, Herta and I go for short walks through the few hundred square feet of forest that separate our house from the cemetery. Insulated from the crowded and dangerous town, the small patch of forest is the one place where we can find some semblance of normality again. We sit and read books to each other. Herta asks about what life was like in Izbica before the war and before her arrival. I tell her about how when I was younger, my mother could barely go anywhere with me because we would always be stopped by people wanting to pinch my cute cheeks. Herta is extremely amused when I describe the circus that I had once set up in our backyard involving ropes for acrobatics, and barn animals such as goats and calves brought by my cousin who was an animal dealer. Herta is also the best and most beautiful audience I have ever had for my singing. My favorite song to perform for her is a rich cantorial piece that my cousin Chaim taught me called "Rachem Na."[1] Herta never fails to become enchanted by its deep melodies. It connects us to our ancestors who sang this prayer for hundreds of years in many distant lands.

I often ask Herta about the far-off places to which she has traveled. I learn that she has been all over Germany and even to several Italian cities and Amsterdam. She describes the life of a German aristocrat and makes fun of how I would blunder at becoming one, that I might say a blessing over pork sausages, or that I might make a name for myself singing the great German operas in Hebrew and Yiddish.

Herta and I laugh the most whenever I tell her stories of the lovable street characters of Izbica, many of whom have already been taken by the Germans.

One townsman everyone had known and loved was named Hersz Lehrer. He had been a teacher, photographer, scholar, philosopher, and comedian all wrapped inside one person. When poor men asked him for something to eat, he would reply, "Do you like Yesterday Stew?" When the poor men had said "Yes," Hersz would say, "Come back tomorrow. I'm cooking it today."

And we all know the story of how, when Hersz was on his deathbed, he had called in his wife and told her to put on her best clothes and jewelry. When she cried, "Why now, when you are so sick?" he had answered, "So that when the angel of death comes, he might like you more than me."

There had been yet another famous character in town, Lipa the water carrier. For people who lived too far from the well, he would carry water to people's homes, with the buckets hanging like scales from a plank of wood across his shoulders. At the High Holy Day services every year, we would say to Lipa, "Hopefully next year you will not need to carry the water all the time." He would respond by saying, "Are you my friend? Do you really want me not to carry the water? What will I do instead? Should I become a thief?"

The storytelling provides some relief from our desperate fear of ending up with our names on the wrong Judenrat list. But the distress never goes away. We believe the stories of what has occurred in Bełżec and the new rumors about another purported killing station, Sobibór. We feel it is still just a matter of time before we all meet our ends—unless a miracle occurs and the Soviets liberate us. Or, as Herta repeatedly assures me, Fritz can save us. But part of me doubts that even Fritz can forestall the inevitable for much longer.

Despite the respite from the transports, our living conditions deteriorate. The town is overcrowded. Sanitary conditions worsen. An epidemic of typhus breaks out, taking many lives.

Toba is apparently afflicted with the dreaded disease. Most of her beautiful hair falls out as a result. Dr. Marienstras puts Symcha in charge of typhus control for the town. Soon afterward, Symcha hands me some spraying equipment along with a white armband that reads "DISINFECTOR." He tells me that the Judenrat will ask me and Dr. Marienstras's son to spray every empty house after its occupants have either died of typhus or been sent to the camps.

"This will protect you from deportation," Symcha says. "Just make sure you wear the armband at all times."

Dr. Marienstras's son and I go house to house, spraying disinfectants. Since Dr. Marienstras's son is originally from Warsaw, he relies on me to lead us to the homes that we are assigned to spray. By going inside the houses and walking about the entire town as freely as we wish, we can now fully comprehend the scale of what the town has experienced. Many entire families have disappeared. Those who have survived are still hopeful—some of the German Jews have even planted beautiful flowers in an attempt to make their new homes more livable—but nearly everyone seems to be deteriorating physically and mentally. When we walk past their homes, their first instinct is to hide, especially when they spy our official-looking armbands through their windows. "Don't worry," we call out to them. "We are just Jews here to spray your neighbor's house for typhus." We spray homes on about ten of the next thirty days. After each day of work, the Judenrat compensates us with small amounts of food.

Despite our best efforts, typhus continues to afflict hundreds of people. It is a horrible disease that causes many of the sick to become mentally deranged. Symcha reports that one patient in the hospital has committed suicide by throwing himself into the outhouse's pit. Because there is not enough room in the small hospital to treat everyone, Symcha also begins visiting people's homes to administer injections of typhus medication. Though Symcha is only a pharmacist, Dr. Marienstras has trained him to treat the typhus sufferers because there are not enough doctors to begin with and even some of them are now dying.

The Germans' deep disdain for the ill displays itself viciously one day, when Symcha comes home visibly shaken and tells us what has happened at the hospital. Uniformed Germans had come and shot at everyone there, including patients, doctors, and nurses. Symcha is one of the few survivors. He had managed to hide under a patient's bed.

In spite of the madness, killings, and disease, Herta confesses a desire to marry, as do I.

My dreams of a future together with Herta are my new reason to continue. Should the nightmare ever end, I will enter into a wonderful life, with a wonderful girl. Good can still exist in the world. "We must tell our parents the good news right away," I say.

Herta agrees. And though neither of us says it, we know why there is no time to waste: nobody knows what tragedies tomorrow might bring. Although we are too young to marry at the moment, we want our parents to at least know our intentions before it is too late.

I am nervous about telling Herta's parents, but they take the news very well, as do my parents. Apparently our silent flirtation has not been as secret as we have thought—our families have suspected for some time.

We expect her parents to hold firm to the tradition of marrying their eldest daughter first, but under the circumstances of such an uncertain future we are allowed to be engaged. Mr. Rosenberger takes me aside and says he will allow it only because he knows how well I have taken care of his family and that this has proved me to be both a *mensch* and deserving of his daughter.[2]

We celebrate quietly that night, not with drink or song, but with a lightened spirit, with talk drunk on the promise of a good future, of any future. And for a few hours everyone's spirit seems genuinely lifted. Idealistic plans are made for my inclusion into their family once "all this mess" is over. I will finish school in Germany. I will go into business with them.

"After the war," Mr. Rosenberger announces, "you will come back to Germany with us, as a member of our family."

In actuality the thought of living in Germany, a nation capable of doing what it is doing to us, repulses me. I feel there is no way I can ever live there. But choosing not to spoil everyone's rare good mood, I keep my reservations to myself.

Symcha teases me: "You'll become a blueblood. You'll bark orders to your workers, and none of them will know you for the matze baker's son you are."

6

Fall 1942

Soon we are sharing our house with even more people: our two cousins, the Luft sisters, who arrive in Izbica after the Nazis liquidate the ghetto in Zamość. Nearly everyone in Zamość, including their parents, have been sent to the camps, but these two beautiful girls, both in their early twenties, have somehow been spared. Before the war these girls, whose family owned a tool factory, had even won a beauty pageant. Now they have been marched with a small group of other Jews from Zamość to Izbica, a distance of about thirteen miles. Many of the weakest Jews had died during the journey.

Now that most of the Jews of nearby Zamość have apparently been killed, everyone in Izbica expects that our turn will follow. The only question is the timing. Every day brings new speculation about when the next—and final—roundup will occur. We talk about it obsessively. The entire town is rife with rumors, some of which turn out to be true, but just as often not. Daily life is an ordeal filled with dread of the beatings, murders, and deportations that we have already seen inflicted on others. People now walk around in a kind of stupor, as if they have been pronounced guilty of a crime but are still waiting to be told what the punishment will entail.

We develop a survival strategy: leave home only when necessary, remain constantly aware of the signs of the beginning of a roundup, and always carry something of value that can be used to bribe a soldier or a policeman. We also attempt to locate and arrange as many hiding places as possible around town, so that in the event of a roundup, we will always have a place to flee to immediately, no matter where we are at the time. Symcha even arranges with one local Catholic family to make their attic available as a hiding place to us. Concealed as it is in a non-Jewish home, it is perhaps the best hideout of all. We know that a treasured hiding place in a home owned by Poles is available to very few Jews in Izbica. First of all, it takes great courage for this Catholic family to offer shelter to us despite the German authorities' warnings that anyone who assists Jews will face the death penalty. Second, unlike most Jews in Izbica, Symcha, thanks to his former role as a dance instructor and his current activities as a pharmacist, has enjoyed unique opportunities to build mutual trust with many local Poles, even since the beginning of the war. Jews who have been brought here from faraway cities and lands have had even fewer chances than Izbica's native Jews to develop connections with the Poles of Izbica. We feel fortunate. But we know that we are still in great danger.

In the middle of October 1942, our worst fears are realized: the transports resume with a vengeance.

Alter is among the first to be caught. When the roundup begins, I head straight for the leather factory. Alter is found, however, before he can find a hiding place. Then he somehow manages to escape from his captors. He seeks shelter in the leather factory. But I listen as he is turned away at the door by the factory's Jewish guard, Jankiel Altman, because there are already too many people inside. I cannot blame Mr. Altman because he is trying to save us. If the Germans were to find us hiding there again, they might not spare us as they had the first time, especially if they were to find people other than workers' immediate families in the factory.

According to witnesses outside, Alter soon had been caught by Schultz, taken to Engels, and shot on the spot.

I am not only sad about Alter. I am enraged. I begin to dream of obtaining a pistol and ambushing Engels and Klemm. I want to avenge the deaths of all my friends and relatives whom they have murdered. I cannot stand being powerless any longer. I know I can very probably be killed trying to carry out my plan, but I feel it is something I must do. Also, if I am really going to be murdered one day soon, then why not at least try to take vengeance while I still can?

I inform my father of what I intend to do.

"Don't be *meshuggah*," he tells me.[1] "Even if you succeed, they will kill you. And who knows what they will do to you—not to mention all of us— before they kill you?"

I start crying. "But they have killed everyone—our family, our friends—and why? Why should they deserve to live?" I yell. "I must do this, and while I would like your help, I do not need your permission."

My father will not answer me.

I know where to obtain a gun. The father of one of my Catholic classmates, who is also a friend of my father, has connections with Polish underground fighters. I believe he can be trusted because he is friendly with my father and he, too, has lost many friends—including the best-educated Poles sent away earlier in the occupation—to the Germans.

I'm not sure how much a gun will cost, but in exchange for the gun I plan to offer a watch and a gold ring that Mr. Rosenberger has given me, but which I have failed to sell. Because I had not been able to find any other buyers, my father had bought both and told me to hold on to them "just in case" we need them.

I nervously walk to my classmate's house and present my offer to his father. After thinking about it for a few seconds, he takes the watch and the ring and requests some leather as well. This is not a problem for me to obtain, because we have hidden some leather from my father's tannery under our roof. I return home and quickly bring back a piece of leather both long and thick enough to produce at least six shoe soles. He promises to bring me a gun.

I wait a few days without hearing from my classmate's father. Then another transport occurs, and several more days pass without any news about the gun. With the transports now becoming so frequent, I waver. Perhaps it will be even more difficult to carry out the plan at this point. But I also suspect that maybe my friend's father has told my father about the deal, and my father has stopped him from giving me the gun. Maybe my father has even paid his friend not to obtain the gun. Knowing my father, I understand that he wants to save me from being killed. And I realize that he is probably right to believe that my plan is reckless. It would truly endanger everyone because of the collective retribution that surely would follow. So I abandon my plan.

But I do not get the chance to ask my father if he has intervened, because another roundup occurs and he is caught up in it. According to our neighbors, he had been taken as he walked down the street. From there, they had brought him to the movie house, which is now encircled with barbed wire and used as a holding station during these roundups. Once they had gathered enough people to fill the cattle cars, they had marched everyone to the train station just a few hundred feet away. Aunt Czypa has also disappeared, leaving her daughter, Hena, to fend for herself.

Our entire family is grief stricken. Symcha is the only one who manages to stay fairly composed. He shows a brave face. Although he is barely thirty years old, he is now our family's oldest man. He has already been a source of strength and protection for all of us, but now I sense these father-like qualities in Symcha all the more.

When Herta sees me crying, she tries to console me. "Everything will be better when the war is all over," she says. "You will come back to Germany with us, and we will have a joyful life together."

"I don't know if I can live in Germany," I confess. "When I see Germans, or when I hear the language spoken, all I can think about is death. We should go to Palestine."

Herta is surprised yet understanding. "We'll see," she says. "Wherever we go, we will be happy together."

We barely have any time to process the latest horrors before roundups occur again, the following day. Back we go into the nearest hiding places we can find, but this time our relatives from Warsaw are captured just outside the house before they are able to enter the hiding places.

A few days later, several people who had disappeared during the round-ups return with news of my father's fate. They say that the day after he had been taken, he had in fact returned to Izbica after jumping from the train through a small window, just a few miles from Bełżec. The people report that he had been limping a little bit but was otherwise uninjured. But he had been spotted by local policemen and taken to the movie house again, where he had told these people his story. From there an entire transport of cattle cars had taken them and my father away. They say the trains had taken them all the way to the village of Sobibór, which they all know from rumors is a place where Jews are being taken and killed. But somehow they had been able to run for their lives when the train reached Sobibór, and they had eventually made it back to Izbica. They are certain that my father and everyone else who had not escaped with them have ended up in Sobibór and are very likely dead.

The next day Mr. Rosenberger follows me outside the house when I go to fetch wood. He hands me a sealed envelope that he says contains detailed instructions of how his assets in Germany are to be handled after the war. My father's disappearance has clearly affected Mr. Rosenberger. For the first time, I can see anxiety expressed on his face. "Fiszel, if something happens to me, you will be in charge," he says. "Take this envelope and bury it in the hiding place."

Even Mr. Rosenberger is losing faith. I do as he has requested, concealing the envelope within the dirt ground of our hiding place.

A few more fearful days pass, and then yet another roundup takes place. We all quickly descend into our respective hiding places: the Rosenbergers below the interior of the house and I along with my mother, two sisters, two cousins, and niece below the ground outside the wall of the house. Symcha is safe in the hospital, we hope.

We wait for about an hour. Just a few minutes after the commotion above subsides, I think I can hear footsteps inside the house. Normally the roundups end after an hour, but to be extra safe we usually stay hidden for another few hours until we can be more certain. But this is an extremely cold day, and it would have been tempting to go back into the house sooner than usual in order to get warm. That would be the only reason why the Rosenbergers would have decided to emerge from their hiding places so soon. We begin debating whether we, too, should come out. But the outcome of our debate is soon settled when we hear people shouting inside the house. Either Germans or their collaborators have stormed inside. Through the din I can hear Herta's cries. After just a few moments, the shouts cannot be heard anymore.

I know that Herta and her family have been taken.

When we finally deem it safe to come out of hiding, we find that the Rosenbergers are indeed gone. Once again the Germans have murdered many, including the girl I love. When will this end? Who can end it? Not even Fritz has been able to save his own family. Perhaps he has been denounced. Perhaps he has been killed in combat. Or perhaps he has been simply powerless to intercede, as I had once heard him say.

I am devastated. But I refuse to feel helpless. I still have my family and my dreams to live for. And I have the power to shut out my feelings. From now on, I will not let myself think about the past, all that I have lost, or why all of this is happening. I will try to focus only on the present. Survival will be minute by minute from now on. I prepare to do whatever is necessary to save my life and the lives of my remaining family members.

7

November 1942 to April 1943

Just a few days later, I leave home to buy food for everyone. A large roundup abruptly begins while I am on the way to the store. I am too far from our hiding place, so I run into a Jewish neighbor's house and hide with a few other people in the closet for about an hour. With dozens of the black-uniformed Ukrainians conducting house-to-house searches on behalf of the Germans, I know we are in trouble. The Ukrainians find us easily enough and march us to the movie house with hundreds of unfortunate others.

We are packed tightly into the barbed-wire area surrounding the movie house. We wait there for what feels like eight to ten hours. We guess that there is not enough room on the trains they have readied for us. The area is so crowded that people are struggling for air. As the night wears on, we all become extremely hungry and thirsty. No one has access to a toilet. The situation is so dire that people begin giving money and jewelry to the guard in exchange for water polluted with kerosene from the nearby river. Then I hear a girl's voice calling, "Fiszele, Fiszele, water."

It is my twenty-year-old cousin Hena, who is normally so vibrant and lively, but who is now driven only by desperate thirst. She seems to be near death. I must do something. The small coins that I had taken with me to buy bread will not be of much use now. But I have a Shafhausen watch that Mr. Rosenberger had given me to use in case of emergency. It is hidden inside a double pocket that my mother had sewn inside my jacket. I tell Hena I'll approach one of the guards and try to bribe him.

I make my way toward the door. It is guarded by a Polish policeman. I show him my watch and offer to give it to him if he frees me and my cousin.

But he simply laughs and says, "Child, where will you go? They will kill you anyway."

Of course I can't tell him that we can go to one of our hiding places. "We don't care," I say. "We will try to manage."

"Do you have another watch?"

"No, just this one is all I have."

He takes the watch and tells me, "Then only you can leave. You won't get far anyway."

I try to stand my ground and plead with him, but I have nothing more to give him, not even at our house. I must leave my cousin behind.

But can I trust this collaborator not to shoot me in the back after I leave? Once again I have little choice but to take the risk. I walk away as calmly as possible, praying that he will not kill me. Only when I am entirely out of his sight do I breathe a little easier.

When I reach home a few minutes later, I find my mother, my two sisters, and my niece. They have all hidden in the Catholic family's attic that Symcha had arranged.

But the Luft sisters are gone.

They had been home when the roundups began. The sliding door to the exterior hiding place is just slightly ajar. Perhaps they had tried to open it, but it had been an extremely cold day and the mechanism could have been jammed by the cold temperature. With only seconds to spare, they could have gone upstairs and hidden under the hay that we keep up there. We examine the attic, and as we have feared, the hay appears to have been moved. They must have been found and taken away.

We hear from the Judenrat that everyone has been taken to Bełżec.

A few days later, yet another akcja begins, and we all descend into our hiding place. My mother becomes very sick with fever. We do our best to comfort her in the cold, cramped pit. We use our urine to make hot compresses for her. But as the day progresses, the roundup does not cease. My mother's condition worsens. Seeing her in pain disturbs everyone. We decide that I should take a chance and go out at nightfall to find some water for my mother and bread for everyone.

Upon emerging from our hiding spot, I find that every room in the house has been ransacked. Feathers are everywhere. Whoever did this had stopped at nothing to find any of our remaining valuables. As I stand there in disbelief, thinking that this is what a pogrom really looks like, a Polish fireman enters the house. Tall and powerful, he begins beating me viciously.

I try to block the fireman's punches without much success. All the while he is yelling: "What are you doing here? Don't you know the town is *Judenrein*?[1] No more Jews allowed!"

The fireman's blows have drawn blood, which is rushing down my face from the top of my head. I can barely see anything. The fireman takes me to a holding area outside the prison where I find about sixty other Jews. They also have been told that the Germans have declared our town Judenrein. This means that Jews are no longer allowed to live in Izbica, and therefore any Jews caught in the town will be killed.

About an hour later, Schultz arrives. He immediately draws his gun and without saying a word shoots the shoe-store owner, who is standing next to me, in the head. Schultz had certainly known the man well. Some of the poor man's blood spatters across my own bloodied face. Then Schultz shoots the man who had run a meat market, again without any warning. I have seen much already in the previous years under German occupation, but I am now beginning to sense what Judenrein really means: this is a new, unforgiving, totally relentless phase of brutality.

Helped by several Ukrainian soldiers, Engels, Klemm, and Schultz march us at gunpoint to the edge of town, in the opposite direction of the train station. I surmise that they are not sending us to a camp like Bełżec because maybe there are not enough of us to justify a full transport by train. But I don't know where they are taking us. Within a few minutes we reach the small hill leading from the main road to the cemetery. I begin to fear that the absolute worst might await us inside the cemetery. As we ascend the hill, another prisoner lunges out of line and attacks one of the armed Ukrainians. I recognize the man as our town's most prominent wrestler, a short but muscular man named Itze Mojsze, who had defeated all comers in competitions before the war. But several Ukrainians quickly rush in and fatally shoot brave Itze Mojsze.

Upon entering the cemetery a minute later, we are forced to stand on wood planks in front of a freshly dug pit. The pit has apparently been created by a few workers who are standing around with shovels. With our backs to the pit, we stare straight ahead at Engels, Klemm, and Schultz. Each of them raises his machine gun and points it directly at us. Surely many of those around me feel that this is the end. But I am thinking only of how to escape the bullets.

Without moving my feet, I begin shifting my weight backward, toward the pit. Then Engels shouts: "Fire!"

At the exact moment that I hear his command, I jump down into the pit. I cover my head as bodies fall on top of me. I move my head just enough to find some air between the bodies over me.

Somehow I am still alive. So are many of the people around me. They are writhing and crying in pain. I don't feel any pain, but I am also covered in blood. I don't know if any of the blood is my own, perhaps from a wound that I can't yet feel.

Above the screams of agony all around me, I can hear the murderers discussing what to do next. They are standing right above the pit, surveying their work. I wonder if they will fire more bullets into the grave to put the living out of their misery. Instead, they say that they should look through the grave for money and valuables. But there is not enough light. They agree to come back in the morning, when they can look for what they want before covering the bodies.

A few minutes after the murderers depart, the cries of the few survivors remain but begin growing fainter. One by one, they bleed to death.

I am in shock. The stench of blood is overwhelming. It reminds me of the cow's blood I had removed from the back of our house a year ago. But the odor that now envelops me is even heavier and more putrid. And I will have to endure it for at least several more hours, until I can be sure that it is safe to escape.

My sense of smell soon grows desensitized. I also begin to recover from my initial shock. I concentrate on listening for the sounds of anyone guarding the site. After several hours of not hearing any voices or movements outside the pit, I feel confident enough to venture upward. It is probably well past midnight by now.

I emerge from the pile of bodies. Just a few of the gravely injured are still moving and groaning, hanging on to life. I want to help them, but there is no way to save them now. I carefully peek over the top of the pit. I don't see anyone. I slowly climb out, and then carefully walk out of the cemetery.

Under the faint moonlight, I pause for a moment to look down at myself. My skin and clothes are soaked in blood from head to toe. I feel as though I have emerged from a slaughterhouse. With my hands I search for wounds anywhere on my body. There are none. Somehow I have managed to avoid the bullets.[2]

But I still must find water and bread. I walk behind a few homes and see that they have all been pillaged. So I go into one of the empty homes and replace my bloody clothes with a women's dress. Then I go to the well near the bus stop, where I wash off the blood as best I can. I also manage to find a pail, which I fill with water to bring back to our hiding place. Then I head to the bakery, named Królikowska, and hide nearby for about an hour until I am able to steal a hot loaf of bread cooling outside the store.

By this time it is nearly dawn. I have been gone from the house for about ten hours—much longer than anyone anticipated. When I return to the hiding place, I knock on the sliding door. They barely have the strength to open it. Everyone is crying. They had heard the shooting coming from the direction of the cemetery and feared that I was dead. When I appear, their sorrow quickly turns to relief and happiness. But my mother looks as if she is near death. I tell them that the whole town has been declared Judenrein. But I choose not to tell them the details of what I have just gone through, for fear that it will overwhelm my mother. All I say is that I had to wait all night for the bread to be put outside the bakery before I could take it.

We are now faced with even more difficult decisions. If the town is really Judenrein, then we can no longer walk the streets or even stay in our homes anymore. All of us—except for perhaps Symcha, who might still be needed to work in the hospital—must find a permanent hiding place. One option is to live in the woods. But we reject this choice because it is winter and it will be difficult for any of us, especially our sick mother, to survive in the forest. Of course, Symcha and I can go together into the woods and perhaps join a group of partisans or find one of the cavelike pits in which we have heard some people are living. But we need to stay and take care of our mother, sisters, and niece. And besides, if one of us is killed in the forest, then the other will be left to face the dangers of the woods on his own. It seems that the soundest decision is to stay together as a family.

The next day Symcha discovers that indeed his utility to the Germans will allow him to remain in town legally. He also learns that because they are supplying leather for boots and coats needed by the Wehrmacht, the Jews who are still working in the leather factory—about twenty-five in all—will be the only other Jews allowed to live.[3]

Without our father to protect us at the leather factory, we must think of a better hiding place. But after considering all our options, we guess that the factory will still be the best place to hide. After all, it is right under the Germans' noses and might thus draw less attention from the Germans during any future roundups and searches. Either we can try to convince the workers to let us work there with them, or we can hide in the factory's large cellar located just outside the factory. The cellar is completely detached from the factory and is normally used for cold storage. Hopefully we can hide there with or without the workers' consent. If anyone is discovered in the cellar, the factory workers can always plead that they didn't know that people were hiding there. Along with my mother, sisters, and niece, we pack a few belongings and some food and head for the factory.

When we arrive, we first try to sneak in. After I lift everyone over a tall wall to enter the grounds of the factory, we attempt to enter the building through one of the back doors. But Mr. Altman and several others block us from entering, just as Alter had been shut out, saying that the Germans allow only a limited number of Jews inside the factory and it is already full.

With the door closed to us, we resort to our second option, the cellar. We successfully descend into the frigid room without being noticed by anyone inside the factory. But once inside, we discover about one hundred other Jews. They too have decided that this will make the best hiding place. I know this situation cannot last long. There are simply too many of us in one place. We are an easy target. Also, we are without food or nearby toilets. It is extremely cold. My mother begins calling out, "Symcha, Symcha, Symcha!" even though Symcha is not even with us.

Being one of the youngest and strongest of the group, at night I am selected to sneak out to steal food from nearby farms. I leave around midnight and collect some food without incident. When I return a few hours later, however, I find the hiding place empty. Apparently, they have all been discovered and taken away. I fear that everyone, including my beloved relatives, is dead.

Having nowhere else to turn, I try my luck inside the factory. I find an enormous barrel—nearly the size of a small room—that is used in the leather-making process. I decide to hide in a groove at the top of the barrel. I can remember that this barrel was once driven in circles by horses, but by now they have been using a motor. Exhausted, I soon fall asleep inside the barrel. When morning arrives, the workers turn on the motor. The barrel begins spinning around. Before it completes a full revolution, it spits me out onto the floor. I am discovered. The Jewish workers tell me I cannot stay because it will jeopardize everyone else. "Where will I go?" I ask. "We don't know," they tell me and shrug. "But there's nothing we can do." And with that, they take me outside and close the door.

I understand why it is necessary for them to send me away, and I don't blame them. On the other hand, I remember what had happened to Alter when he was in this situation. To survive I must think fast and find some-place to hide.

I remember hearing about a good hiding place in the Bejt Jaakow not far away, where I once hid in the closet. There is a large oven on the top floor of the building. People sometimes hide inside this oven. So I hastily walk there, climb the stairs quietly, and enter the room with the oven. When I open the oven door, I find four men already inside. Luckily there is still room for another, and even better, all the guys are friends of Symcha and Jakub!

I am optimistic about our chances in the oven. We spend the entire next day there. But at night we need to find food. The stairs of the build-ing are lit only by a few traces of moonlight. We descend as carefully and quietly as we can. But with darkness and a day's worth of hunger to con-tend with, my balance and concentration are impaired. I lose my footing on the staircase and tumble headfirst down at least half a flight of stairs. I land on my back. But aside from a few bruises, I am not seriously hurt, and I actually feel lucky because I have not broken any bones. At a time when I need to walk more than ever, it seems almost as though my legs have adapted; they are like steel.

We find food by approaching local farmers whom we believe we can trust and telling them we are partisans. A few farmers freely give whatever they can to us. From other farmers we steal vegetables from their barns at night as well as salamis that are hanging there.

We repeat this process several times over the next few weeks. Then one night in early December, a farmer tells us that the Germans have posted proclamations throughout a fifteen-mile radius of Izbica stating, in both German and Polish, that Jews are allowed to live in Izbica again. Instead of being Judenrein, Izbica is now a *Judenstadt*.[4]

We know exactly what the Germans are up to. Many Jews have undoubtedly been forced to hide in the woods while Izbica has been Judenrein. But there are already heavy snowfalls, and very few people will survive the winter without decent shelter over their heads. The Germans know this and are therefore luring us back to Izbica so that they can collect us in one place, the easier to kill us. Everyone knows this is the Germans' intention, but there is no choice. People are desperate. Almost no one can bear living in the woods during the harsh winter months.[5]

I go back to the leather factory immediately because I think that Jews might likely concentrate there. Sure enough, there I find Symcha . . . and my sisters and niece! They have all been living in the woods until now and are still suffering from severe frostbite. Their limbs are blackened in some places due to lack of circulation.

Brancha and Toba describe how, along with Sara, they have survived because that night in the cellar of the leather factory, my mother had convinced them to seek a safer hiding place inside the leather factory. She herself was too sick to sneak in, but my sisters and niece had successfully entered the building just before the cellar had been discovered. My sisters say that later that night, they had heard shots and screams from the cemetery.

"Fiszele," says Brancha in a soft voice, "we are almost sure that Mother was shot along with all the others from the hiding place."

I begin weeping and refuse to accept Brancha's story.

"But she might still be alive," I plead. "The shots could have been fired for other reasons. They could have sent her to a labor camp."

But I know the terrible truth. Izbica had been Judenrein when my mother was caught. And she had been much too old for a labor camp. Much too old to be of any use to the Germans.

"Let us say *kaddish* together," Symcha says.[6]

After we recite the prayer, Symcha tells me what has happened in the hospital. He says the Germans had come and shot all the patients. He had escaped by hiding under one of the beds and then running into the forest with as many supplies as he could find. There he had found our sisters as well as Golda.

Over the next days, we estimate that about one thousand other Jews have returned to Izbica from their various hiding places. Everyone else is gone. No one expects the Germans not to strike again.

Despite the risk of impending roundups, we take advantage of the calm moments to walk around when necessary. We find that Izbica's Jewish neighborhood is now an enclosed ghetto. One can legally enter or leave the ghetto only through a checkpoint where several guards control a long gate fashioned from a single wood pole. There are ways to easily escape the ghetto through unguarded areas, but the risk of being captured or killed by collaborators outside the ghetto is so high that no one dares venture out. We hear that the Germans have promised any person a reward of five zlotys or a kilo of sugar for each Jew captured and turned over beyond the ghetto limits.[7]

The Judenrat gives us assignments to work in our new ghetto, dismantling houses for firewood and doing other odd jobs perhaps intended more to keep us weary than to achieve any specific goal. One day I am assigned to tear down a house, along with Jankiel Pelc. It is hard work, but I quickly learn that even a sturdy home can be completely dismantled in just three or four hours. When we remove the roof, I find a stash of jewelry and Soviet coins. I give it all to Jankiel, because he is older than me. Later he divides everything that I have found with Symcha.

When not assigned to work, we prepare feverishly to save ourselves. Symcha begins trying to arrange for fake identification papers, with Christian names, for my two blue-eyed, blonde sisters. With such documents, they will be able to flee to safety in Germany, where they can find work. Some members of the Polish underground with whom Symcha is friendly have promised to obtain the documents, presumably belonging to women who have recently died. I wish that I too could assume a new identity and flee Izbica, but with my darker features I appear far less Aryan than my sisters. And my circumcision can also land me in trouble.

While we are waiting for my sisters' documents to arrive, an alternative solution is offered to Toba. A member of the Pelc family, Josel, who is a tailor working for room and board at various homes in a nearby village, offers to take Toba to live with him. Even though he is Jewish, the villagers both like him and need him, so they don't report him to the Germans. Josel is a very good man, and he has never made a secret of his desire to woo and marry Toba. But Symcha will not allow Toba to go. He feels that the false identification papers offer a better and more honorable chance at survival.

We also begin digging a new hiding place connected to the leather factory. The entrance will be through the factory, but a tunnel will connect to a pit beneath a Catholic family's nearby property. Several fake walls will be installed to effectively conceal the hiding place. And the location beneath the Catholic family's property is all the more attractive because in the event of a roundup, the Germans will search far less intensively near the homes of Poles than near our homes or the factory itself. We also plan to install many tubes to bring air into the tunnel. Along with several other townspeople, we set to work digging the tunnel for hours upon hours, day after day, night after night.

In January, with the new hiding place not close to being ready, another roundup occurs just as we have feared it would. This time Golda disappears. She has been hiding in an underground pit that Symcha had created for her. But perhaps on this occasion she had not made it to the hiding place in time. The next day Symcha asks a local Pole who works near the Gestapo's main office if he knows anything about her fate. The man tells Symcha that he had heard the sounds of Engels, Schultz, and other Germans raping her. When they were done, they had shot her to death.

Several weeks later the Germans order a new roundup. Anyone without a good hiding place is captured. People are either placed on a rail transport to the camps or simply machine-gunned in the middle of town. Hundreds of people are massacred at once. Even Rabbi Landau is captured along with his two sons. He has managed to survive until now. Although the synagogue had long since been closed, he had continued to comfort everyone by leading *minyans* in the homes of people who are in mourning.[8] He had even officiated at several weddings and circumcisions or sent delegates when he could not attend himself. Our desperation now grows. We live with the total fear of knowing that time is very quickly running out. We fully expect to be taken away soon.

During these gruesome days, there are also random shootings. One afternoon I am home with Symcha when a teenaged boy from Czechoslovakia is brought to our door. He has been shot and is bleeding severely. Symcha believes that the wound is mortal. There is nothing we can do but sit with him and provide him with company in his last moments. He tells us that one of his parents is Jewish. Over the course of five hours, he cries and asks for water to quench his thirst. We provide whatever comfort we can before he finally bleeds to death.

Our hopes for survival are buoyed in April 1943 by news of an uprising by Jews in the Warsaw Ghetto. Apparently, the Germans have begun liquidating that ghetto, and the people there are fighting back. These Jews in Warsaw have inflicted casualties on the mighty German armed forces. This makes me feel good, and more importantly, I am sure that it has made it easier for these Jews to go to their own deaths. Even if all of them are to die in the uneven battle, I admire them for being able to take some degree of vengeance. We briefly consider staging an uprising of our own in Izbica, but we have little access to weapons and even less knowledge of how to use them. Why had we not listened to Jabotinsky when he told us to learn how to shoot? Finally, with only a few hundred people remaining—many of whom are weakened by illness and hunger—we will be far outnumbered no matter what resistance we offer. Hiding seems to be our only option for survival.

One day Dr. Marienstras's son, who had been both my friend and partner in disinfecting houses, arrives in Izbica with a Gestapo man. Because Symcha had been the doctor's right-hand man in Izbica, they have remained in contact since the doctor was sent to work in a labor camp called Trawniki, about twenty miles from Izbica. We know that thousands of prisoners, including the doctor and his son, are carrying out various jobs in this camp. When we see the Gestapo man and the doctor's son approaching the entrance to the ghetto, we quickly flee to the nearly finished hiding place by the leather factory. They immediately proceed to our house. Finding it empty, they then go to the leather factory, apparently because they know our family is in the leather business and we might be there. We hear them calling, "Symcha, Symcha." They tell the people in the factory's office that they have come to take Symcha to Trawniki, where the doctor is requesting Symcha's full-time assistance. Life may not be easy there, but at least it can present us with a chance to live if Symcha can take us with him. Here is our opportunity to escape from Izbica! But Symcha doesn't utter a word. He does not want to take any chances. Even if the doctor truly wants to save Symcha, going to Trawniki is not at all safe. Though it is a labor camp, we strongly believe that the Germans plan to eventually kill every Jew whom they can. We remain in our hiding place. The Gestapo man and the doctor's son give up their search and return to Trawniki.

Day and night, we continue constructing the hiding place connected to the leather factory. When the eight days of Passover arrive in April, instead of baking the matze as we have done for years before the war, we invest all our energy into finishing the hiding place. By the end of the festival, the hiding place is nearly complete. We have dug out a long tunnel and a large chamber under the Catholic family's property. However, it is still not perfectly concealed, and we have not added tubes for air yet.

In the early hours of the morning after the Passover holiday ends, we are awakened by gunshots coming from outside the house. The Germans have declared the town Judenrein once more, and Jews are being rounded up. Symcha, Brancha, Toba, Sara, and I have no choice but to flee to the still-unfinished hiding place. We make it there without being seen, as do about one hundred other people who crowd into the tight space with us.

The Germans of course know that many Jews have returned to Izbica. But when they arrive at our houses, they find no one because most Jews are hiding somewhere away from their homes, just like us. The Germans concentrate their search in the leather factory. We hope that our hiding place will conceal us, but in truth we know it is just a matter of time before they find us or before we must come out for food, water, and air.

We remain hidden for several hours. Slowly it becomes more and more difficult to breathe. The cries of several babies cannot be stopped. From inside the hiding place, we can hear axes breaking down walls in the leather factory. Soon the axes reach our wall, and we are found by about six Poles who are apparently collaborating with the Germans. They order us out.

We have no choice but to comply. When we emerge into the light, we are directed by several waiting Germans to put our hands above our heads, as if we are fierce resistance fighters. One of the Germans takes Symcha's stethoscope from his neck and hits him across the face with it. Then, with our hands still raised skyward, we are marched through the streets. Some women onlookers clap and yell, "Bravo!" I see a few Poles on all fours, with their ears to the ground, listening rabidly for their last remaining Jewish neighbors.

Upon reaching the market square, we are led to two empty trucks that seem to be waiting for us. It appears that most, if not all, of the town's last remaining Jews are already assembled in front of the trucks. There are about three hundred of us. Most of us board the trucks. A few others are taken to the cemetery; we later hear shots from its direction. Either there is not enough room on the trucks, or these people have refused to go.

The convoy begins heading north. The direction of Sobibór.

We ride for over an hour before we reach Trawniki. The trucks stop at the entrance to the camp. We are all comforted by the knowledge that at least we are not at Sobibór. We will need to work at Trawniki, but at least we will live a little longer than if we had ended up at Sobibór.

The SS man steps down from the front of our truck. He walks into the camp's office. After about fifteen long minutes, he comes out and steps back onto the truck. Then, abruptly, we drive off. We guess that the SS man has tried to drop us off at Trawniki, but they must not have wanted to accept us. Again we are traveling north. Now we all know we must be on our way to Sobibór.

Symcha and I begin quietly discussing what to do when we arrive at Sobibór. We can't jump from the truck, because then they will probably kill us and perhaps everyone else. Maybe we can attack the guards, depending on how many we find at the camp. After two hours of riding, we still have not settled on a realistic plan. The trucks halt in the middle of a pine forest. We step down from the truck near a train-station house with a sign that reads "SS Sonderkommando Sobibór."[9] It is April 28, 1943.

8

Life in Sobibór

We have heard from people who had fled the areas near Sobibór and Bełżec that the camps in these places are killing centers. Nevertheless, part of me has not wanted to believe their stories. Now I am here at Sobibór. A tall barbed-wire fence stands before us. We are surrounded by black-uniformed Ukrainians, and beyond them stands the deep forest. Flowers, trees, grass, and a nicely paved road appear to mark the camp's entrance gate. I certainly haven't expected a death camp to be decorated so attentively, but this does nothing to assuage my fear. Surely this is the place where our father and so many others from Izbica have been taken and never heard from again.

Everything begins to make sense: if the Germans want to murder us quietly, this is the perfect place to commit the crime, in the middle of nowhere. Part of me thinks that, after all the experiences I've suffered through, at least this will be my end. No more hunger. No more fear. No more watching the deaths of my friends and family. Finally, I will have some peace. But at the same time, I tell myself, I am only a teenager. I want to live. I want with all my heart to live.

We are standing on the sandy ground of a receiving area alongside the railroad tracks. Escape is an impossibility, for we are watched not only by the armed Ukrainians but also by several SS officers and a huge guard dog.

Once everyone has exited the trucks, an SS officer calls out, "Are there any professionals or tradespeople? Doctors, dentists, pharmacists, plumbers, mechanics, electricians, shoemakers, tailors, step forward!"

One of the main lessons we have learned since the beginning of the war is that it is always good to be useful. My brother, clever and quick as always, senses our chance. He immediately grabs my hand and drags me out from the crowd. The officer asks Symcha to state his profession. Symcha replies that he is a pharmacist and that I am his assistant. The officer nods in approval and tells us to stand to the side. In this manner a few dozen other people are also selected.

I know that my older brother has just saved my life.

We are almost certain that those not selected, including Brancha, Toba, and Sara, are marked for death. With tears in our eyes, we say good-bye for the last time. Even my seven-year-old niece cries when she hugs me, knowing that she will be killed.

Along with the other selectees, Symcha and I are led into the camp. Each of us is aware that the other might be his only relative left alive. My and Symcha's survival are what matters most to me right now. Though he does not express it in words, I know that Symcha must feel the same way. To survive this ordeal, we must continue doing all that we can to protect each other.

The camp appears at first glance to have a perimeter of about one to two miles. There are about fifty small- to medium-sized single-story buildings, all within a triple-rowed, barbed-wire fence surrounding the camp. Watchtowers manned by armed Ukrainian guards are located at intervals along the fence. Interior barbed-wire fences divide the camp into several subareas. We are given clothing, a blanket, a bowl, and a spoon by a Jewish foreman called a *kapo*. This kapo is apparently one of several prisoners selected by the Germans to oversee other prisoners. He wears a special armband and cap. Although he is friendly to us, we assume he is a traitor, given that he also carries a whip. The kapo then escorts us to our wooden bunk beds in the prisoners' barracks. There we wait, uncertain of what comes next, until dozens and then several hundred prisoners begin arriving in the square outside the barracks. Though they appear to be tired, they also seem to be relatively healthy and well fed. A tiny glimmer of hope appears. Can this be a work camp after all?

We venture outside, where we notice a dense, foul-smelling fog that has enveloped the camp. We approach the nearest prisoner and eagerly ask what is going on here. He answers our question with a question.

"Did you arrive with anyone else?"

"Yes," we tell him. "We came here with our two sisters and our niece."

Then the prisoner says, "It is very difficult for me to explain what is going on here. But this is a death camp. The Germans have killed tens of thousands of Jews here so far. The big flame that you see burning on the edge of the camp and the fog all around us are from the crematorium — that is what is happening to every transport that arrives here."

I already knew that they have been killed. But now I watch their funeral. The repulsive odor carried by the fog can be nothing but that of burning human flesh. Symcha and I embrace each other, crying. We pray the kaddish.

"Be strong," Symcha tells me.

I know it will be difficult to face whatever awaits. But by caring for each other, we will still have something tangible to live for despite the loss of our beloved relatives. And by looking out for each other, I tell myself, we will help each other survive.

Lunch, consisting only of a bowl of watery soup, is served. Everyone lines up with bowls and eats the food standing up. Now is our first chance to meet the several hundred other "lucky" prisoners who have been spared from death, at least temporarily, because the Germans have selected them to help operate this death camp. For these veteran prisoners, we represent an important opportunity to learn news of the outside world. We find a neighbor from Izbica who has been in the camp for several months. "What happened in Izbica?" he wants to know, and we tell him what has become of everyone. "How close are the Soviets?" he asks next. We do not know, but we are able to at least deliver the good news of the ghetto uprising in Warsaw.

We ask for our neighbor's advice on how to survive in Sobibór. He informs us that, according to a few of the veteran prisoners, the camp is about one year old. There are about six hundred prisoners in the camp at all times, he says. They work for a period of time either until the daily brutality of the Ukrainian and German staff results in their deaths or until they are singled out for murder and replaced by new prisoners. The schedule for rotating prisoners is unpredictable, but it is apparent that the Germans do not want people to gain too much knowledge of the camp.

The interior fences divide the camp into three distinct zones: Camp 1, Camp 2, and Camp 3.[1] Most of all, our neighbor tells us, we should avoid at all costs the area near Camp 3. This is where the gas chamber is housed. Between 100 and 150 prisoners live and work there under close guard. The Germans enforce strict secrecy about what is occurring in Camp 3. No contact at all is permitted between Camp 3's prisoners and the prisoners from our sections, Camp 1 and Camp 2. The Germans are so obsessed with maintaining secrecy that anyone who so much as catches a glimpse inside Camp 3 is taken to the gas chambers. In the past, our neighbor says, several workers have been killed after simply delivering food or supplies to Camp 3. Anyone too ill or too injured to work is also routinely sent to Camp 3 to be killed.

Next we want to know if anyone is planning an escape. The neighbor says that of course people think incessantly about escaping, and that one or two people may have even succeeded at sneaking away from the camp in the past. But he tells us to look at the numerous obstacles. On the other side of the barbed-wire fences that surround the camp, a field of land mines separates us from the forest. Guards with machine guns monitor us at all times from the watchtowers. And the neighbor informs us of the great danger of even mentioning to anyone that we are thinking about escape: yesterday about seventy Dutch Jewish prisoners were murdered in connection with an escape plot that was apparently revealed by an informant. They were ordered forward at roll call and marched to Camp 3, where they were shot. Only two Dutchmen were spared. One of them is a painter named Max van Dam, whom the Germans value for his ability to provide artwork for them and their wives.

If this story is true, I think to myself, then I owe my life not just to Symcha but to a group of brave Dutch Jews whom I have never met. Had the Germans not needed to replace the workers whom they had just killed, they never would have selected any workers from the trucks in which we had arrived.

Despite the ongoing killings of prisoners, a few veterans have somehow managed to survive, often because they are skilled workers who cannot be easily replaced. Before explaining any more details, however, our neighbor pauses. He takes a deep breath and tells us that he feels obligated to tell us something. "I cut your sister Toba's hair before she went to the gas chamber," he says. "She recognized me and asked, 'How long will the gas take to kill us?' But I couldn't answer her, because we are forbidden from talking to anyone in the haircutting area."

This information is too much for Symcha and me to handle. We cry together once more. But we do not blame our neighbor for telling us. It is important for us to know, rather than speculate, how our sisters and niece spent their last moments.

Still unassigned to work, we return to the barracks until evening. Every prisoner lines up in rows. The kapos count us one by one, and then report the evening's inventory to several presiding SS officers, who then check the numbers against their records. Each prisoner is given hot water and a few slices of *Schwarzbrot*, which we are informed will need to last us through the evening.[2] We are also informed that we can look forward to a cup of coffee and a slightly larger serving of bread in the morning. We expect to be hungry.

Between dinner and evening curfew, we have a few hours to socialize within Camp I. Ours is one of two men's barracks, which stand side by side. The women have their own barracks, separated from the men's barracks by a building that holds the prisoners' kitchen. These buildings face a small courtyard surrounded by several other buildings, including workshops for tailors, shoemakers, carpenters, and painters. In the barracks and the courtyard, I observe people playing music, singing, dancing, and flirting. It is terribly much for me to process on this first evening. However, I feel encouraged by the knowledge that for at least a few hours of each day at Sobibór, I will be able to let my guard down and perhaps enjoy life again in some way.

We sleep in bunks beside each other. Above us rests my friend Toivi, who has come with us from Izbica. During the day I had mostly managed to keep my mind occupied with every new challenge. But when I lie in the bunk, my thoughts turn to each of my murdered relatives and friends. I wake up in the middle of the night many times screaming out their names. Then I realize I am not alone in my sorrow. Other men are also groaning, screaming, and crying.

In the morning we awake at 4:00 a.m. with the rest of the prisoners and wash ourselves using the sinks situated outside the barracks. After we receive our breakfast, jobs are assigned. Symcha is sent to the workshop where confiscated medications and perfumes are stored, and I am sent along with several dozen other prisoners to the sorting shed. There I find mountains of suitcases, bags, and loose clothing. Each prisoner takes a station, and I receive instructions from the supervising German officer on how to sort the belongings. Jackets to the jackets bin, shoes to the shoes bin, and so on. Naturally the Germans know that their victims often hid valuable items—such as coins, paper money, diamonds, emeralds, and rubies—anywhere possible, but especially inside their clothing and shoes. I am ordered to search carefully for these valuables and to place them in a special basket. I understand that all these plundered items had belonged to the recently murdered. Their belongings will obviously be used to somehow support the German war effort. Being new to the job, I am warned by the German officer that he will search the items after they are sorted, and if he finds any valuables in items I have previously searched, he will consider it an "act of sabotage" and I will be killed. I quickly learn how to easily feel for hidden valuables inside garments. I even learn that if I find a loaf of bread, I can cut it open and often find jewels baked inside.

The kapos overseeing us ensure that we work briskly. When Germans are watching, the kapos are especially vigilant, sometimes even using their whips on us. Aside from dealing with these random outbursts, however, the work is fairly easy. Until I come upon a dress and a blouse that look familiar. They are similar to a dress and a blouse that Herta had often worn. I raise the blouse to my nose to see if I can still smell any of her perfume. A faint but recognizable scent remains. Whether it is really Herta's clothing or not, the effect is the same. I am overcome with emotion. I think of her hand holding mine. Her voice telling me how much she wants me to be her husband. Our final kiss. I can barely go on with the work, but I do so by telling myself that she would have wanted me to live. So would my parents, so would my sisters, and so would all my friends.

At night Symcha tells me that he has spent the day classifying and arranging the medications on hand in the pharmacy. His pharmacy is shared with another area where valuable medical instruments are brought. Other professionals have informed him that their services are needed only irregularly in the camp—usually after large transports of Jews—so they are often put to work at whatever other jobs the Germans assign, such as sorting belongings or felling trees. Because a pharmacist is more valuable to the Germans than a worker who can only sort clothing or chop wood, Symcha tells me he will request that the kapos assign me to his workshop whenever there is enough work to be done. Again my older brother is doing everything he can to protect me.

Within days transports of Jews begin arriving by train, and I quickly learn the details of the routine killing process of the camp. The camp is overseen by between ten and twenty SS officers. In addition to them, about one hundred to two hundred Ukrainian soldiers man the watchtowers and gates and guard the work details. The transports come frequently—on average, several times per week. The arrivals are always Jews. Mostly they come from either Holland or Poland. Their origin influences their manner of death.

The Dutch Jews arrive on passenger trains. They are nicely dressed, well fed, and still carry most of their valuable belongings. Every available seat on their trains is filled, which means that typically anywhere from one thousand to three thousand people arrive at once. A group of about twenty prisoners called the *Bahnhofkommando* is called by the kapos to meet the passengers at the station and assist with removing their heavy baggage from the trains.[3] These prisoners don neat blue overalls and caps. Though I am not a regular member of the Bahnhofkommando, I am occasionally ordered to assist this group by working as a porter during particularly large transports.

After I have helped the Dutch Jews with their bags, many of them offer me a tip for my services! My heart is bleeding, because I know that in a half hour the human being standing in front of me is going to become nothing but ashes. I want so much to warn them, to tell them to throw themselves on the guards and escape, but it will not do any good. They probably would not believe the story I have to tell them.

A few of the arrivals are unable to walk because they are either elderly or disabled. These Jews are asked to remain behind at the platform. They are ultimately loaded onto small, iron rail carts, which carry them along a specially built track for about three hundred yards to Camp 3, where they will be killed. But first the Germans carry out the rest of their carefully planned deception on the other new arrivals.

The Dutch Jews appear to have no inkling of what awaits them. The Germans have thoroughly duped these people into believing that Sobibór is a bona fide resettlement camp. The lie is initially reinforced by the neat and colorful village amid a thick pine forest, which they behold from one side of the train: flowers, gravel paths, and quaint homes with red roofs and pleasant names like "Lustiger Floh," "Gottes Heimat," and "Schwalbennest."[4] After such a long journey from their homeland (it would have taken them at least two or three days and nights of rail travel to cover the distance of more than a thousand miles from Holland), they probably want very much to believe the mirage. To these new arrivals, the young and relatively healthy Jews like me—working in ostensibly pleasant conditions and greeting them politely—are probably interpreted as a sign of positive things to come.

Everyone is told to leave his or her heavy luggage behind. Then a column of men and women carrying babies, with children following, are walked through a barbed-wire alley toward a long barracks. There they are ordered to leave their purses and small hand luggage, which they still carry. Here a few become uncooperative. Their private papers, money, jewelry, and medicines are inside, and they hesitate to part with their important and precious articles. The Germans actually try polite explanation, telling the prisoners that they can pick up their bags later. But whenever that fails to bring results, the Jews are beaten mercilessly. Despite the beatings, the prisoners still do not suspect what awaits them. After all, they have surely seen beatings before. And the process is moving so rapidly that they barely have a chance to think and perhaps recognize what is taking place.

The moment the barracks are empty, a group of prisoners—which includes me on a regular basis—converge and remove the bags to an adjoining warehouse, where we sort them and search for valuable items in the following days. The Germans urge us to move the baggage out of the barracks as quickly as possible so that the next group of victims can be processed. They shout at us, "Run, run!" I am strong enough to run with the bags, but some of the weaker prisoners are not. The exertion causes some of them to fall to the ground. Whenever this happens, the nearest guard descends upon the fallen prisoner and whips him until he returns to his feet.

Meanwhile, the Dutch Jews are led rapidly to an enclosed, partly covered yard. Here they are welcomed in a steady and friendly voice by an SS officer. I usually hear him beginning his speech with the same firm but polite words, "Quiet, quiet!" Then he sympathetically apologizes to everyone for the inconvenience in travel and for the fact that they cannot go immediately to their quarters to relax. First, for sanitary reasons, he says, they must take a shower and be disinfected. He strongly recommends that they pick up the waiting postcards and write home to their loved ones in Holland reassuring them of their health and resettlement in a decent place. The SS man's speech produces its intended results. The Dutch Jews clap their hands and some even yell, "Bravo!" They eagerly fill out the postcards—the very same cards that some of them must have already received from their loved ones and that must have helped deceive them into compliantly boarding the "resettlement" train in Holland.

After the postcards are collected, a polite order is given to undress. When ready, they are led from the undressing yard to an alley lined with barbed wire and vegetation so that no one can see inside or out of it. The camp's prisoners refer to this alley as "the Tube," and the Germans call it the *Himmelstrasse*.[5] At the entrance stands a kiosk where a German collects watches and jewelry from those passing by, either calling out a number to each victim that he or she is supposed to remember on return from the "showers" or giving the person useless numbered receipts for pick-up on return. This is the last that many of us prisoners will ever see of these condemned people. Another one of my regular tasks, however, is to cut the hair of women on their next and last stop before the gas chamber.

The haircutting shed is located along the Tube, about one hundred yards down the path that the prisoners travel from the undressing yard. It is connected to the gas chambers by a corridor. The first time I am selected to work as a haircutter, it is SS Oberscharführer Karl Frenzel who chooses me.[6] Other prisoners have warned me about Frenzel, saying he is one of Sobibór's most sadistic officers. At first Frenzel does not tell me what I am being selected for. He simply marches me and about twenty other boys toward Camp 3. As we walk closer and closer to the gas chambers, I become increasingly fearful that we have been selected for death. When we arrive at the haircutting shed, we find a room containing two rows of long wooden benches. Frenzel lines us up behind the benches and distributes scissors to each of us. He then says to us, "Women will enter this room, and you will cut their hair. You must work quickly. Do not say anything at all to these women, or you will be punished."

Despite Frenzel's instructions, I remain convinced that we are certain to die. We are within just a few yards of the gas chambers. From what everyone has said, nobody who gets this close to the killing process ever lives to tell about it. I'm nearly paralyzed with the fear that after I cut the women's hair, I will surely be forced to follow the victims to the gas chambers.

Completely naked women enter the shed. Feeling cold as well as ashamed, they cover their bodies with their hands. Frenzel asks them to be seated and apologetically informs them that they must now have their hair cut for the sake of hygiene. One of the experienced haircutters demonstrates the proper technique for the newcomers. The barber takes one lady's hair in his hands and shows us how to cut quickly and without causing injury to the women or ourselves. Once we get started, everything moves like an assembly line. Working as fast as I can, I cut the hair of dozens of women within the span of just minutes. A tense silence prevails throughout, except when either Frenzel or a second SS officer shouts, "Fast, faster!" or when they assure the women not to worry because their hair will grow back very soon. Still believing that they will live, some of the Dutch girls and women innocently ask me not to cut their hair too short. Some of them ask where they are going. I can't answer because Frenzel and the other officer are standing right there, watching closely.

The naked women, now without most of their hair, are then ordered to exit through a different door from the one through which they have entered. This is the door that admits the doomed into the corridor leading to what most of them still believe are the "showers." Hundreds of women at a time pass through the haircutting shed in this manner.

When the last woman's hair has been cut, a floor full of hair remains. We collect the hair and place it in bags. We think the hair will be somehow reused by the Germans (and later on our belief is confirmed when we are asked to help prepare the hair for shipment away from the camp).[7] Now I expect to be led to the gas chambers. Instead, we are marched back to Camp 1. But I am still in too much shock to feel any sense of relief. In just a few minutes from now all these women and girls are going to perish, and I have been helpless to either warn them or save them. Their faces haunt me.

Throughout the camp we soon hear the roar of a motor, mixed with a horrible mass scream that subsides gradually. If another group of victims— either additional women or the men and boys who have arrived with the women—is bound for the gas chambers after the women, then at this point they are on their way to the undressing yard for the same deceptive speech. The mass scream may have alarmed them, but they cannot suspect its cause, so they do not panic. Sometimes the mass scream is accompanied by the honking sounds of geese, which have apparently been frightened by the screams of the victims. After approximately fifteen to thirty minutes, a contrasting silence takes over the camp.

Polish Jews sent to Sobibór meet the same end as the Dutch Jews. But the killing process differs. The contrast begins with their journey to the camp. Based on the stories about Sobibór that many of them have by now heard, these Polish Jews know—just as I have known—that they will be killed. Their cattle cars enter the camp under heavy guard. In many of the train wagons in which they arrive, boards or windows have been clearly damaged during people's attempts to jump from the trains, just as my father had once done on his way to Bełżec. Some people have even smuggled tools onto the train to cut through the bars that cover the windows.

The Polish Jews travel the same path as the Dutch Jews from train station to courtyard to gas chamber. But the Germans dispense with the ruse practiced upon the Dutch Jews and treat the Polish Jews in a more overtly brutal manner. Perhaps anticipating the unpleasantness of dealing with these large and potentially noncompliant groups of Jews, some of the Germans and Ukrainians appear under the influence of alcohol when these transports arrive. Their speech becomes slurred, and they stagger when they walk. But their impairment only serves to heighten their savagery. Many of the Polish Jews are beaten from the moment they step down from the cattle cars or in some cases from the moment they refuse to depart from the cars. These Jews often try to resist the Germans in any way possible.

For example, sometimes there is chaos as Polish Jews attempt to flee from the camp right after descending from the cattle cars. But they are boxed in by guards and barbed wire and are always shot immediately.

When the Polish Jews (and sometimes the Dutch Jews, too) are forced to undress, they often leave behind gold, diamonds, and jewelry beneath the sandy soil of the undressing yard. I find these valuables whenever I am ordered to clear the clothing bundles and rake the sand after the condemned depart for the gas chambers. We are always watched closely by the Germans and Ukrainians and must turn everything over to them. On one occasion I hear a strange noise coming from a bundle of clothes in the yard. When I look closer, I find a baby hidden inside the bundle. She has a pacifier in her mouth and the name "Ada" stitched on her little dress. There is also a note tucked into her dress, written in Polish: "*Save my baby!*"[8] I don't know what to do. So I go to the nearest kapo, Pożycki, and tell him there is a baby among the clothes. He picks up the girl and takes her away. Even if he wants to save her, there is nothing he can do. He has probably taken the baby to Camp 3.

For the Polish Jewish victims, the final indignity of having their hair cut short is, for many of them, too much to take. Some of them cry and refuse to allow it. For this they are whipped by the Germans until they comply. Like Toba before them, many simply cry and ask us if the gas will be painful. From the terrifying screams that I have heard coming from the gas chambers, I know that it will be. But I cannot do anything except continue working in silence. If I utter a single word to them, I can be forced to accompany them into the gas chambers. All I can hope for is to live another hour or day before my turn to die eventually comes. And so I continue working.

One day a transport of passengers arrives from the east in cattle cars. The Bahnhofkommando apparently cannot handle the load on its own, so I and several other male prisoners are selected by Frenzel to assist. He takes us to the train tracks where the cattle cars sit. The order to unload is given. I expect that I am going to simply help the people down from the cars. But when we open the doors, we are immediately enveloped by the stench of decomposing bodies. Inside the boxcars half the people are dead and swollen. There are several babies who look like adults because their stomachs are horribly distended. The people who are still alive are starving and severely deranged. I guess that this trainload of Jews had tried to escape en route to Sobibór and the Germans had either subdued them with some kind of poison gas or simply locked them in the train cars for an extended period.[9]

In spite of the unbearable smell, we must begin helping the few survivors down from the train. One of them, an extremely emaciated woman, must be dragged from one of the boxcars by our group. Her will to live is so strong that she cries out, "Jews! So I have been saved." Despite being in such pitiful and helpless condition, she and the other survivors are brutally beaten and shot by several German officers and Ukrainian guards.

Next we must remove the decaying corpses. I try to pull a dead woman from the train, but her skin comes away in my hands. I turn and see a woman with a baby on top of her. Both are dead and terribly swollen. They are still embracing each other. I stand motionless, staring at them in shock.

I can take no more of this life in hell.

I make my decision: I prefer to die rather than continue with this horrendous work. Hoping that it will force one of the Germans to shoot me, I lie down on the ground. Frenzel immediately approaches and begins lashing me with his whip. "Return to what you were doing!" he yells.

I plead with him that I can't take the smell.

"Here, smoke this while you work!" Frenzel says, while thrusting a cigarette into my mouth and laughing at his own sick joke. Then he catches a glimpse of the woman with the baby on top of her. He quips, "What beautiful scenery," before snapping a photo and walking away. Apparently he hasn't needed to kill me in order to be satisfied.

I carry on. We place all the corpses, as well as the unconscious and semiconscious people, on the small rail carts that go straight to Camp 3.

My experience with Frenzel teaches me that he will be just as dangerous a psychopath as any member of Izbica's fearsome trio of Engels, Klemm, and Schultz. My next encounter with Frenzel comes a few days later when I am bringing a bag to Symcha's work area. I find a salami sandwich in the bag and try to quickly consume the food while I am carrying the bag. Ever observant, Frenzel notices my chewing and sentences me to twenty-five lashes of the whip at the evening roll call.

I have now been in Sobibór for almost a month. Somehow I've become accustomed to the grotesque sight of people being whipped even more brutally than animals. I have known all along that eventually my turn will come. Now that the day has finally arrived, I try to mentally prepare myself by rehearsing what will happen and what I will need to do to survive. As I have learned is the custom in the camp, I will be required to lower my pants so that my naked bottom is exposed to either Frenzel or the kapo whom Frenzel will select to carry out the punishment. The whip to be used will be the standard one that each SS officer and kapo carries with him at all times, always at the ready. Each whip is made of four or five leather straps, about 2.5 feet in length, which have been sewn together. I will need to count out each lash of the whip or else risk being beaten to death, as I have seen happen to other prisoners. I'll also need to pick myself up and walk away after receiving the lashes. As I have witnessed, prisoners who are rendered unconscious or unable to walk by the severe punishment are immediately taken away to Camp 3, never to be seen again. Sometimes their departure is followed by the sound of a single gunshot in the distance. This we know is the sound of their execution.

As I complete my work in the sorting shed that afternoon, I know that just minutes remain before I face the whip. I try again to concentrate on preparing for what awaits. But now all I can think about is why this is even happening. First I blame myself for provoking Frenzel. Then I blame myself for being naive enough to have once believed that we live on a civilized continent. At Sobibór I am witnessing the tools of the modern age— trains, assembly lines, and gas engines—used by the Germans to efficiently murder thousands of people on any given day. And yet how new is this really? Despite all the new technology at Sobibór, the primitive whips used by the Germans are no different from those used by brutal slave masters for thousands of years. Every year during Passover I have grown up reading the biblical story of how Jews had suffered as slaves in ancient Egypt. Why are we enslaved once again? Why is history repeating itself now? Are Jews always condemned to suffer? No, I tell myself, this will one day change when we gain a state of our own in Palestine. Many Jews have already made it to Palestine, and more are sure to follow despite what we are now experiencing at the hands of the Germans. This hope for the future of my people, even if I will not live to be a part of it, gives me the strength I need to face and withstand my punishment. I will accept my lashes just as my ancestors had in Egypt, with the certainty of knowing that I might die, but my nation will not.

At the roll call, I tell Symcha what is in store for me. I can see that he is very worried, but we both feel that I have the strength to withstand the punishment. It turns out to be Frenzel who inflicts my lashes. When the first lash breaks through my skin, the pain is more horrible than any I've ever experienced. My skin feels as though it's on fire. I try to focus on calling out the number of each lash instead of thinking about the pain. Somehow I manage to count out each one of the lashes—"One! Two! Three! Four!" and so on—even though each lash burns more than the one before. When the ordeal finally ends, I draw upon whatever is left of my will and strength to walk away. Otherwise, I tell myself, I will be killed.

Symcha tends to my wounds in the evening. I can sense that he is proud of me. I have passed a test. I have survived. And almost as important, I have learned that I can endure anything, even whatever the next day brings at Sobibór. Thanks to Symcha's expert care, my wounds heal after a few days. But until then I cannot sit down because of the pain, and I can only sleep if I lie on my stomach.

The Germans maintain a special area for burning the documents of the Jews they have gassed. This area is normally manned by my friend Toivi. One morning I am ordered to substitute for Toivi because he is too sick to work that day. The task is more grueling than I have expected. I must continuously feed the hot fire, throwing in endless piles of passports, visas, identification papers, and even books of Jewish study. I had been taught in heder that it is sacrilege to burn a piece of paper that has the name of God written on it—instead, Jewish law teaches that these papers must be buried—but I have no choice. I also tell myself that these documents and photos are the last proof of how these people lived and my hands are the last to touch these testaments to their lives. I resolve to not allow the Germans to completely erase these people from the earth. I will look at as many of the photos as I can so that at least these people can live on in my memories. The eyes and the smiles in the photos each tell unique, beautiful stories that take my mind off this difficult work.

My daydreaming comes to an abrupt end, however, when several hours after the start of my shift, Frenzel drops in to check on my progress. He takes one look at the fire and yells, "It is too high!" Then he tells me to go to a nearby bench to receive twenty-five lashes of his whip. I have barely healed from his last beating. Again I must count out each painful lash. But this time I am a veteran who knows what to expect and knows what I am capable of enduring. Again I survive.

Another of the cruelest German officers is SS Oberscharführer Hubert Gomerski. He derives great satisfaction from using his whip every day. I learn about his sadism first from Symcha, who tells me one evening at roll call that Gomerski had entered the medical warehouse earlier in the day and asked Symcha for some kind of opiate. Symcha had told Gomerski that there was not currently any of this drug in the warehouse, and to please check again tomorrow. Gomerski had responded by giving Symcha twenty-five lashes.

One day Gomerski approaches me in the sorting warehouse and asks for jewelry. But I don't have any because a few hours previously I have given some to Frenzel. I can't tell Gomerski that I have just given whatever I had to Frenzel, because if Frenzel hears that I've informed another officer about his misconduct, he may kill me. So I tell Gomerski that I'm sorry, but I haven't found any jewelry today. Gomerski punches me in the face with his powerful fist. Then he says, "Tomorrow make sure you have a package of jewelry prepared for me, because I am going on vacation. Otherwise I will take you to Camp 3." When he leaves, some of my friends bring me cold water to put on my face. The next day I make sure to ready Gomerski's package. As promised he returns for his jewelry. With my face still swollen, I hand him the package. I am thus spared a second beating. But my face remains black and blue for three days.

As cruel as both Frenzel and Gomerski are, the sadism of the SS officers reaches its pinnacle in the form of SS Oberscharführer Gustav Wagner. He is young, tall, blond, and strong—the most stereotypically Aryan of any German I've ever seen. Wagner's combination of physical strength, intelligence, and brutality make him the most formidable of all the SS men at the camp. We fear him even more than any of the Nazis we have left behind in Izbica. Wagner is a true sadist, a monster who seeks both every reason and no reason to beat us, sometimes to death. He is always dangerous, but especially when he is in a bad mood because then he is sure to find a new victim on whom to vent his frustrations.

Wagner demands that all tasks be performed according to his strict but also arbitrary standards. He frequently walks the grounds of the camp, vigilantly enforcing the camp's rules. Sometimes he even stands outside the walls of our barracks, eavesdropping on our conversations. We are constantly preoccupied with avoiding him. Even when we are simply walking from one part of the camp to another, we always try to consider where Wagner is and attempt to keep our distance. It is not only the prisoners who fear Wagner. The German officers and the Ukrainian personnel both appear very tense in Wagner's presence, and sometimes I even notice them carefully walking away from any areas that Wagner approaches.

One evening Symcha tells me how Wagner had selected him to join the *Waldkommando*.[10] This group of prisoners had been sent to the woods with axes and saws to cut down trees and chop the wood that was probably necessary to fuel Camp 3's crematorium. At one point the prisoners had cut through nearly the entire trunk of a very tall tree. But just before they could finish, Wagner had ordered Symcha and several other prisoners to climb the trees and tie a rope near the top branches. This rope could be used to pull down the tree and thus save a small amount of time. But right after they placed the rope, Wagner had forced the remaining prisoners to pull the rope while the people were still in the tree. The tree had toppled down with Symcha and several others perched on the branches. Every prisoner had hung on to the branches as best he could. Several had lost their lives in the tree. Others had broken bones, which itself is a death sentence because now they will be killed for being unable to work. But Symcha has somehow escaped with only some scratches and bruises.

Wagner is also greedy. Often he brings me to the sandy area in which Jews are forced to undress right before entering the Tube. Wagner knows that some of these people hide their valuables in the sand in their final act of defiance; he knows that we normally find these items—often including gold, diamonds, and jewelry—either when we clear out the clothing from the yard or when we rake the sand; and he knows that we turn over any found valuables to the Germans and Ukrainians. But he is also smart enough to know that sometimes there are items buried more deeply. When nobody else is around, Wagner orders me to crawl on all fours to sift carefully through the sand. He instructs me to dig with my hands a little deeper into the sand than the rakes have gone. I find all kinds of diamonds and jewels and turn them all over to Wagner. There are also brightly colored papers that have been shredded to pieces. The papers are clearly money. Each tiny piece of paper represents a final act of defiance. I am happy in knowing both that the Germans will not derive any benefit from these monies and that the people they had murdered have died with the satisfaction of depriving the Germans of their last savings. On the other hand, I fear that Wagner will kill me after doing this work for him because he may see that as the easiest way to prevent me from reporting to his commanding officer that he is stealing from the German war machine. For some reason, however, he spares me.

We must also fear being whipped by the chief kapo, a young Polish Jew named Mojsze Sturm. Referred to by everyone as "Governor General," he is no more than twenty years old but wields the power both to kill and to save. He has many opportunities to ease our suffering by either making our jobs easier or looking the other way when we transgress the rules. Sometimes he actually helps us but just as often he punishes us, especially if he knows that Germans are watching him. We can never predict how he will use his authority because it seems that not even Mojsze himself knows how he will react to a situation until it actually happens. He is in a very precarious position, always making difficult choices under the scrutiny of all the camp's SS men. If the Germans ever judge that he is not being strict enough with us, it can cost him his life. But because he is so close to me in age, one night I muster the courage to plead with him, "Mojsze, could you please be a little more lenient on us?"

"I am suffering more than you," answers Mojsze, "because I was given more responsibility. I didn't want this job."

I know that I cannot blame him. I am not in his shoes.

Both during and after the transports, my most frequent job is to sort through confiscated property in the sorting shed. The astronomical value of the jewels in the outside world means nothing to me, but while I work I keep my mind occupied by thinking of how the jewels must have looked on the human beings who had once worn them, and how these people might have obtained these special items—through what business successes, through what romances, and so on. Along with jewels and currencies, the documents and photographs continue to tell stories as well. When I don't initially know the origin country of the transport, it always becomes clear from the victims' belongings.

I am supposed to place the jewelry that I find in the jewelry bins, which when full are emptied into a large safe. But because I don't want to contribute to the German war machine, I go to the outhouse whenever I can and throw away some of the jewels. Or if I find paper money, I hide it inside whatever documents I can find and then place it all in the documents bin, the contents of which I know will be burned by Toivi. In this manner I am able to get some satisfaction even though I know my days are numbered. Everywhere we are keeping some of the most valuable spoils of war away from the Nazis. We are quietly resisting, and this feels good.

Most of the prisoners are adults from either Poland or Holland. There are a few other teenage boys like me from Poland who have naturally become my friends in the camp because we can communicate with one another in Yiddish. One of these friends is Szlome Lerer, who cares for the horses in the stables. Sometimes I envy Szlome because his position is not physically demanding and the SS officers are likely to protect him from harm as long as he keeps their cherished horses happy. But Szlome is also one of the few prisoners who must interact directly with the officers every day, and this makes him extremely vulnerable to their deadly whims. Even though I believe that we will all be killed one day, weighing the relative safety of each job at least helps to sustain me; it reminds me that I still want to live despite what I am seeing.

On Sundays an orchestra composed of prisoners plays for everyone. This, the Germans must hope, will enable us to go on with work and not think about resistance. One day the musicians are accompanied by a beautiful Dutch Jew who is a cabaret singer. Her voice is exquisite. She sings high and low notes like an opera singer. My love of cantorial melodies makes me appreciate her talent all the more. I am enamored of her voice. So are the SS personnel, all of whom applaud her performances enthusiastically. She

sings one rather catchy song that immediately becomes a favorite of everyone in the camp. It is an upbeat tune called "Overal, Overal!" whose lyrics
are:

> En dat we toffe jongens zijn
> dat willen we we-e-ten
> daarom komen wij, daarom komen wij
> en dat we toffe jongens zijn
> dat willen we we-e-ten
> daarom komen wij—overal!
> (Refrain)
> Overal! Overal!
> Waar de meisjes zijn, waar de meisjes zijn.
> Overal! overal!
> Waar de meisjes zijn daar is het bal![11]

Whenever we march to and from work, the kapos lead us in military
formation and order us to sing. Sometimes the Germans force us to sing
marching tunes laced with anti-Semitic lyrics. But after the Dutch singer
arrives, the Germans allow the work groups to often sing "Overal, Overal!"
The majority of the prisoners—myself included—have no inkling of what
the song's Dutch lyrics might mean.[12] But the melody lifts our spirits
nonetheless. Only a few weeks after she arrives, however, the lovely Dutch
singer is singled out and killed by the Germans. The rumor is that one of
the SS officers had taken a romantic interest in her, and his comrades
would not allow this.

When the orchestra plays, the men and women are encouraged to
dance. This, too, the Germans must hope will keep our minds occupied
with matters other than resistance. But not knowing how to dance, I feel
unable to approach the pretty girls at these events or elsewhere. And I still
miss Herta.

Then, one sunny day in June, a beautiful Polish Jew who is about my
age begins working at the station next to mine in the sorting shed. I have
noticed her around the camp before but have been too shy to even approach her. She is a bit shorter than me, with strikingly beautiful green

eyes and straight black hair. I stand next to her, grasping for something to say. Then, much to my surprise and delight, she takes the initiative. "What is your name?" she asks.

"Fiszel," I answer nervously.

"That's a cute name," she says with a bemused look on her face. Her name is Rosa. We continue with our work, but exchange glances and smiles every few minutes.

"I'd like to talk to you more," she whispers softly to me at the end of our shift. "Come and meet me this evening in the yard."

My heart flutters for the first time in many months. I find Rosa that evening sitting in the yard. It is a warm evening, and she looks even more beautiful than ever. We begin talking about how we have survived so far in Sobibór. She had not volunteered to work as my brother had done. Rather, an observant officer had saved her because, said the German, "Sobibór needs more pretty girls." I tell her that this is the only thing I can agree with the Germans on. We share a nice laugh together.

The more we talk with each other, the more I understand that Rosa is not just a pretty face; she is also very intelligent and sensitive. She confides to me that she wants to live because she is the only one left from her family. Everyone else has perished at Sobibór.

"I've lost nearly everyone, too," I say.

We kiss and soon become Sobibór's newest couple.

"If we survive this place," Rosa tells me, "we will be together and build a new generation of Białowiczs."

I cannot think of a better dream to have.

Rosa invites me to meet her in the women's barracks next time. Several of the friends I've made since arriving at the camp have told me that they often visit their girlfriends in the women's barracks. Even though it is forbidden for men to be in the women's barracks, the Germans allow it— probably because they believe it will give us just enough hope to continue working for them. Men thus frequently sneak in and out of the women's barracks to visit their girlfriends. Sometimes they make love there. My blood races with nervous excitement.

I decide to wait a few days before visiting Rosa in the barracks. I want to impress her, and to do this I find it necessary to bring her some presents.

My parents had taught me never to arrive empty-handed at someone else's home, and I think this rule should apply even to the barracks in Sobibór. So I wait a few days until I can take some sardines and chocolates from the packages of the Dutch Jews who have recently arrived. I also wait for a certain Ukrainian guard who is known to barter with the prisoners. He routinely enters the sorting shed and asks for money in exchange for any food and alcohol that he can provide. I have never dared to engage in this risky game before—if I am ever caught with the smuggled food, I can be whipped again or killed—but the thought of impressing Rosa sufficiently emboldens me. I also remind myself that I have no chance of surviving Sobibór. Either I will die now, or I will die later. If my death at Sobibór is guaranteed, what difference will it make if I am killed for engaging in this strictly prohibited trading with the Ukrainian? At least the food can help keep me and Rosa healthy enough to live another day.

When the Ukrainian guard walks past, I make eye contact with him. He smells the opportunity. "Give me some gold," he says, "and I will bring you salami and vodka."

I quickly hand several Soviet coins to the Ukrainian and tell him, "I would appreciate whatever you can provide, and next time I will give you more."

Two days later the Ukrainian returns to the sorting shed with both the vodka and the salami. He gives them to me and says that next time he would prefer that I give him diamonds. I agree to his request, not caring at all whether I give him gold or diamonds. Both are worthless to me except for the food and drink they can fetch and either can get me killed if I am caught stealing them. The Ukrainian promises to return in a few weeks.

When I bring the presents to Rosa, I can see how happy she is to receive them. We share the gifts with each other and her bunk mates. One of them teases us with a Yiddish saying: "Love is sweet, but tastes better with bread."

I ask Rosa to tell me what she had dreamed of doing before the war began. She says she had wanted to be a legal assistant. Of course we have both been in Sobibór long enough to know that we do not have a professional future ahead of us. We will surely die soon. But we are alive for the moment, and this is enough to keep us going. Rosa and I are soon spending every evening together in the women's barracks. I love her, and she loves me in return.

Every few weeks there is an evening when the prisoners are allowed to make music and dance with one another. It's a form of entertainment for the Germans, who stand around clapping and singing while some of the prisoners try to dance despite the pain we all feel. I have always been too shy to dance with anyone. But I know that Rosa loves to dance. Sure enough, as soon as the music starts to play, she grabs me by the hand. "I don't know how," I plead. "But I thought Symcha was a dance instructor," she says playfully. I tell her that I had always been too young to learn from him then. "Don't worry," Rosa says. "I'll show you." She shows me the steps and gently leads me through the first few dances. Within a few minutes I have learned how to waltz.

Knowing that Symcha is a pharmacist, Rosa one day asks if I can obtain two bottles of poison for us to ingest if the Germans ever send us both to Camp 3. We know that men and women are gassed separately. Instead of dying alone, she says, it would be better to commit double suicide. "We will face death together," she says. I don't want to even think about this scenario, but in my heart I agree with Rosa's plan. So I ask Symcha for the poison, and he gives it to us. We hide the bottles by our beds. We don't dare discuss it any further, but I think we both know that even if only one of us is ever selected for the gas chambers, we will still take the poison together. Dying in love will represent our final victory over our murderers.

One day while Rosa and I are working in the sorting shed, a friend of mine named Mordechaj, who comes from the town of Żołkiewka, asks if I can give him a package of groceries that I have found in the hand baggage of Dutch Jews. Mordechaj and I have become good friends in the camp because we have had similar upbringings in small Polish towns and he sleeps in the barracks bunk below me. So I think nothing of giving him the first food I can find: a wrapped package that I can see contains some sardines. But after I covertly hand him the small package, I look out the window and see Frenzel stop Mordechaj in his tracks. I feel as helpless and terrified as I had felt the day that Fritz first came to our house. Not only can Mordechaj be killed if Frenzel finds the package, but I can be killed, too. I watch in horror as the scene unfolds, each second seeming like an eternity. Frenzel searches each of Mordechaj's pockets. He finds the package, takes it, looks inside, and finds the sardines. Then Frenzel appears to ask my friend where he has gotten the contraband. Mordechaj gives a short reply that I cannot hear. Frenzel immediately begins leading my friend in the direction of the kiosk in which I am working. Can Frenzel know that the package came from my kiosk? If so, he will surely kill me. I decide to hide. The only place I can go without arousing suspicion is the outhouse. I quickly relocate there and wait for several very tense minutes. Then a kapo's voice can be heard on the megaphone: "Fiszel Białowicz, report to the sorting shed immediately. Fiszel Białowicz, report to the sorting shed immediately."

Now I really believe it is the end of my life. Frenzel must have figured out that I am the culprit, or maybe my friend has betrayed me. Even worse, there is the chance that Frenzel will opt not to shoot me but rather to torture me to set an example for others who would consider doing what I have done. I consider killing myself. I can throw myself into the pit of the outhouse. Would it be preferable to the torture I am about to endure? But after all I have been through, I can't give up now. I decide to return and face whatever consequences await. If my punishment is death, I will resign myself to it, but not until the very last moment.

I walk to the sorting shed in a daze. When I arrive there, I find all my coworkers standing in a group around Frenzel and Mordechaj. My friend is shaking all over his body. Frenzel asks Mordechaj: "Who gave this to you?"

Mordechaj manages to compose himself for a moment and answers: "I sneaked inside the shed and stole it by myself."

With these few words, my friend has just saved my life and possibly the lives of the other workers. Frenzel leads Mordechaj away toward Camp 3. Several minutes later we hear the sound of gunshots. A half hour later, according to what my friends in the nearby sorting barracks tell me, my friend's clothing had arrived for sorting.

As I stare that night at the bunk beneath me where Mordechaj had once slept, I can't stop thinking of the heroism that my friend had displayed. He had been tested under the most extreme circumstances, and he had responded by setting an example for everyone to follow. I resolve to be grateful to Mordechaj and to bless his memory for the rest of my life. And when word of his bravery spreads to everyone in the camp, it surely inspires others as well.

Until now I have continued the risky game of trading valuables for food several times per week. A willing Ukrainian guard can always be found. Whatever I receive—usually salami, sardines, or vodka—I share with Symcha, Rosa, and our friends in the barracks. I also provide stolen food from the sorting barracks to a few of the religious Jews who need the sustenance more than anyone because they choose not to eat their daily ration of soup, which is made with non-kasher horsemeat. They gladly accept sardines as well as cheese from Holland. Whenever I give food to these religious Jews, they bless me. But after seeing what happened to Mordechaj, I stop trading with the Ukrainians once and for all. I begin to worry that if I am ever caught, the Germans will torture me until I name the Ukrainian with whom I am trading. But I will continue to take from the warehouse. Food is vital for everyone's health at Sobibór. Without enough of it, we can fall ill or become too weak to work and the Germans will kill us. And at least nobody else can be punished if I am caught stealing food on my own.

One day Frenzel escorts me and a small group of workers to the nearby town of Włodawa to dismantle brick houses. We assume that the Germans will use these bricks either to expand the camp or to support the cremation of the bodies of those who have been gassed. My position is on a balcony. I am told to stand there and stack the bricks that the others are removing from the roof and passing to me. From the balcony I have a clear view of our surroundings as well as of the position of Frenzel and the few Ukrainian guards assisting him. We are right next to the woods. At a certain moment I look up from my work and cannot see either Frenzel or the guards. This means they also cannot see me. If I act now, I can descend from the balcony and run into the forest, to freedom. I judge that with a head start of only a few seconds, I can outrun the guards and escape from Sobibór.

But, I think to myself, what will happen to everyone else? All of them, including Symcha and Rosa, will likely be tortured or killed as punishment for not preventing my escape. My character cannot allow me to desert them like this. These are all the people who matter most to me in the world. Everyone has grown close during our time in Sobibór. If we are to die, I want us to all die together. If we are to live, I want us to all live together.

I carry on with my work stacking bricks atop the balcony. After I amass what seems like hundreds of bricks, the entire balcony collapses under the huge weight. I fall with the balcony and the bricks to the ground about ten feet below. When I realize that I am not dead, I am incredibly relieved. However, one of my legs is in terrible pain. I look up and see Frenzel pointing a gun at me. "Stand up!" he shouts. I know what this means. If I cannot get up, I will be of no further use at Sobibór, and he will shoot me on this very spot. I take a split second to pray that my leg is not broken. Then I jump up. The pain in my leg is excruciating, but thank God I am able to stand. Frenzel orders me to clean up the bricks.

I work through the pain for several more hours. Then, at the end of the day, two of my friends help me walk back from the truck to our barracks. Once there Symcha administers some painkilling medication and brings a Jewish medic to examine me. He says I'll be fine, but that I should not walk on the leg for at least a day. Now we have another problem: if I don't go to work tomorrow, then I will be severely punished, if not killed. Luckily, Symcha is friendly with one of the kapos. He convinces the kapo to arrange for me to be given a job cleaning the barracks the next day. There are three boys whose normal job is to clean the barracks. The kapo arranges for one of these boys to trade jobs with me for the day. So I hide in my bunk all day. I cover myself with blankets and leave a small space to breathe. The two other cleaners do my work for me and keep watch for any Germans or Ukrainians approaching the barracks. The boys plan to warn me if anyone approaches, and if time permits, I will try to jump out of the bunk and begin cleaning. Luckily nobody checks on us. After the one day of rest, I am only partially healed. But Symcha feels that it is too risky for me to stay in the barracks beyond one day. I agree and manage to return to work the following day.

A few weeks later Wagner takes me and a group of prisoners to empty all the water from the well. Sometimes this is done when the water develops a foul odor; other times it seems to us that the water is fine and the Germans are simply forcing us to exert ourselves with pointless physical activity. On this particular day I am among the prisoners standing nearest to Wagner when he calls for volunteers, so I have no choice but to show my willingness. To work under Wagner's scrutiny always means the real possibility of being beaten or killed. But as he escorts me and five other prisoners to the well, we realize that our lives are in even more jeopardy than usual, because Wagner's face is sallow and he is acting strangely. He is perhaps drunk. At the well he forces me and two other boys—one from Poland and one from Holland—to climb down to the bottom of the shaft, using two ladders fastened to each other with rope. As we send up several metal pails filled with water, he orders us to send them faster. We process the buckets as quickly as we can, but nothing is good enough for Wagner. He takes the empty pails and mightily throws them down the well at us. The buckets strike our heads, and within seconds we are bleeding profusely. For the next fifteen horrible minutes, we send up pails full of bloodied water as Wagner relentlessly rains the buckets down on us, pail after bloody pail. Then it is the next prisoners' turn. This goes on for several hours until Wagner's drunken rage abates and his sadism is sated. I have not been this bloody since the night I had crawled out of the mass grave in Izbica. But this time the blood includes my own. The moment we are released, I thank God that Wagner has not killed us.

When I return to the barracks, I am still bleeding from my head. Symcha quickly procures iodine and bandages for me. Rosa arrives and starts crying at the sight of me. She tends to my wounds and eventually the bleeding stops.

Later that night, Rosa tells me: "Our relationship makes it easier for me to live in Sobibór. Being with you, Fiszel, makes me think about life instead of death."

9 | Planning Vengeance

Many prisoners simply cannot stand the atrocities that they witness every day. Some commit suicide. This is itself a form of resistance because they die on their own terms and they deny their labor to the Germans. But many other prisoners, confident they will also be killed no matter what, feel compelled to do more than work for the Germans. Like me they sabotage the Germans whenever possible. And more important, these prisoners—including me—are becoming obsessed with vengeance. Our hatred for the camp's personnel grows with each passing day. If we can somehow escape, this would mean the victory of survival. But even more than surviving, we want to take vengeance. We live for the chance to avenge our dead relatives and friends.

In late June an unusual transport of Jews arrives. When they step down from the train cars, the prisoners all throw themselves upon the guards in the unloading area. We know this because throughout the camp we can hear chaotic shouts and gunshots in the unloading area. When we sort through their belongings, we find notes telling us who they are. Their messages to us state: "We were all prisoners in Bełżec. The Germans used us to close down the camp and told us we were being sent to a work camp in Germany. The Germans even gave us provisions for the trip. But now we are arriving at Sobibór, and we know this is the end of our journey. We see that we will meet the same fate as our brothers and sisters. You too will be killed. Do not be fooled as we were! Take vengeance! Take vengeance!"

I and the others who work in the sorting shed take the notes and distribute them to our friends. Before long everyone in the camp has read these notes. The prisoners of Bełżec provide inspiration to us. Many of us resolve to focus our energies on finding a way to escape, for if Bełżec is closing down then Sobibór can be next, and we will indeed suffer the same fate as the Bełżec prisoners.

Our fears of liquidation only worsen when the transports begin arriving at less frequent intervals in July. People begin thinking even more seriously of any way to save themselves or to at least take some measure of vengeance before the Germans kill us.

Near the end of July, I am working in the sorting shed when I hear shots ring out in the distance. At evening roll call, I learn why the gunshots occurred: according to the kapos, several prisoners from the Waldkommando escaped while working in the woods! But my happiness for the escapees is short-lived, because the Germans quickly order the entire camp to march in the direction of Camp 3. Now we think that surely the Germans are going to kill us all. Prisoners begin whispering to one another in Yiddish, "Vengeance, vengeance."[1] We are all unready to be killed without putting up a fight. If it appears that the Germans are about to shoot us, we will rush at them and try to take their weapons. We will have very little chance of saving our lives, but we will have nothing to lose at that point and maybe we can succeed in taking some vengeance.

After we arrive at a yard just outside Camp 3, the Germans bring in the remaining prisoners from the work detail in the woods. A few are already dead. The others, eleven Polish Jews, are made to crawl into the yard on all fours. They are covered in blood and look severely beaten. Some are shaking. We are forced to form a semicircle around them. Wagner announces, "These foolish prisoners tried to escape today. And now they are going to pay for it. There is no escape from Sobibór! This shall be your fate if you do the same foolish thing that these prisoners did." Then the Germans and Ukrainians take aim at all the workers. Right before the "Fire!" command is issued, one of the condemned men, an older prisoner who had arrived with me on the trucks from Izbica, shouts his final words to us: "Take vengeance!"[2]

The shots ring out. The men fall to the ground in front of our eyes. After a few moments, one of the men begins to rise up from among the lifeless bodies. He has somehow survived the firing squad. Frenzel immediately approaches and shoots the man to death.

We learn the next day that a Ukrainian guard had been killed by the prisoners during the escape. When he had taken two of them to fetch water, they had used their axes to kill him and then had run away into the forest. When his death was discovered by the other guards, some of them had gone to search for the missing Jews. Seeing the confusion of the guards, several Polish Jews had seen their chance and fled as well. The Dutch Jews among the group had chosen to stay put, knowing that their lack of knowledge of both the countryside and the Polish language would severely hinder their chances of survival in the forest outside Sobibór. At least five of the forty prisoners in the Waldkommando had succeeded in escaping from Sobibór.

At night in the barracks we discuss how these Jews who escaped had caused the deaths of their fellow prisoners and had endangered all of us. Had this been right? I don't think so. They had not been true fighters. They had wanted only to save themselves, no matter the consequence for everyone else. This is very wrong. I myself had had the opportunity to escape when they had taken us to dismantle those houses in Włodawa, but I had chosen not to because I had known it would jeopardize the lives of all my friends. I also could have escaped one day when I had been doing some gardening near the unloading platform and our Ukrainian guard left us to get a drink. But again I had decided it was not the right thing to do.

On the other hand, these escapees at least prove to us that escape from Sobibór is indeed possible. This is important because it gives us hope. Many of us have already been thinking of ways to escape, but until now we have never known if success is really possible. These prisoners show us that there are certainly weaknesses at the camp that we can exploit. And even if we fail, we will die bravely as the Jews of the Waldkommando have done and we will avenge their deaths.

One warm August evening at roll call, Symcha returns from work bleeding all over his body. He has been whipped without mercy. "Wagner almost killed me just now," Symcha announces.

As I already know, Wagner needs only the smallest pretext to kill, and if one is not readily available, he is always adept at creating one. Symcha knows this just as well as I do. So, I ask myself, how can he have been so foolish as to attract Wagner's attention?

Symcha begins explaining what has occurred. "Last June," he says, "I approached Hersz, the boy from Zamość who works in the Germans' kitchen. I told him I had devised a way to poison their food. I asked for his help."

"You tried to poison the Germans?" I ask with a mix of disbelief and admiration.

Yes, Symcha confirms. He says that only he and a few others have known about the risky plot. "For the last two months," Symcha now reveals, "I was secretly removing morphine from the bottles that people had brought with them on the transports. Whenever a 500 milliliter bottle came in, I placed 200 milliliters of the morphine into a large, unlabeled bottle that I kept hidden in the pharmacy and then wrote '300' on the original bottle and on the inventory. I removed the morphine drop by drop, day after day, until the large bottle had enough to kill all the Germans and the Ukrainians. It took a long time, but I did it."

Now he begins shaking his head. "We had enough. We had enough to kill all of them. Then we would steal their weapons and everyone would escape."

"So what happened next?" I ask.

Symcha says that Hersz had recruited a girl who worked in the Ukrainians' kitchen. She would poison their lunch on the same day as Hersz would poison the Germans' lunch. Hersz had told Symcha that she was a strong girl and that she could be trusted to do the job. "So last night," Symcha continues, "I transferred all the morphine into empty vodka bottles, one bottle for Hersz and one for the girl. When I gave Hersz the bottles, I told him, 'Be careful. If either of you gets caught with these, tell them you found these in the sorting shed.'"

"It should have happened today," Symcha says. Instead, Wagner had brought the vodka bottles, along with Hersz and the girl, back to Symcha's workshop. Symcha had thought he was going to surely die. Wagner had immediately begun beating Symcha with his whip and yelling, "Filthy Jew, you thought you could kill us? Nobody kills us!" Symcha had tried to explain that he had never seen the bottle before. That vodka bottles are never kept in the medical warehouse. That someone must have stolen the bottle from the sorting shed. Symcha had pled with Wagner, "All my bottles are labeled and accounted for, all my bottles are labeled and accounted for." Symcha had even grabbed the inventory and showed it to him while the beating continued. But this was Wagner. He wouldn't listen to a word that Symcha had said. He had known that Symcha was lying. Finally Wagner had pointed his gun at Symcha and announced that Symcha would die for his mistake.

"At that moment," Symcha says, "the SS officer who supervises the pharmacy walked in and saw me on the ground, about to be killed. This SS man was a pharmacist himself. He asked, 'What is this?' After Wagner explained everything, my supervisor came to my defense! He said it was impossible for the poison to have come from his shop, because everything was meticulously inventoried."

Symcha doubts that his supervisor really felt this way. More likely he had just wanted to keep Symcha alive because he wished to avoid the trouble of finding and training a new worker. Or he may have been trying to save his own skin after appearing to have allowed poison to escape from an area he controlled. Whatever the reason, he had saved Symcha's life. Wagner had placed his gun back in his holster and walked away with Hersz and the girl. Symcha says he is sure that both of them have been executed.

Hersz and the girl do not show up at roll call or later in the barracks. We must assume that they have indeed been killed. Through a Ukrainian guard, we hear that Hersz's female accomplice had been betrayed by a Ukrainian whom she had tried to save from her poison. Apparently, he had once told her that a fellow guard had fled from Sobibór and had taken with him a Jewish girl from the camp. He had expressed his belief that this other guard had done a good thing by escaping from Sobibór and saving a Jewish girl at the same time. Feeling that the guard telling the story sympathized with the Jewish prisoners and wanted to escape Sobibór himself, the girl had then warned him, "Don't eat lunch tomorrow." The girl's naïveté and compassion had cost both her and Hersz their lives.

Despite their failure, the young conspirators have left their mark on me. Plots of intricate resistance—involving more than simply running for our lives when working outside the camp's barbed wire—now seem increasingly realistic. I know that I am one of the youngest in the camp. But if Hersz and this girl, who were both teenagers like me, could risk their lives so bravely to take vengeance and possibly save themselves and others, then why can't I? I long for nothing more than to avenge the deaths of all my family members and friends. And although I need to keep Symcha's story a secret from others—because if too many people find out, then it really can endanger his life—I know of many others who share my obsession with vengeance. And with so many people intent on vengeance, I am starting to really believe that we can achieve something.

Late one night we are roused from our beds and marched out from the barracks into the yard. As we stand half-naked in the warm night air, we look around at dozens of Germans and Ukrainians pointing machine guns at us. We can hear shots in the distance, coming from near the minefields. The next day Frenzel tells us that "bandits" had tried to approach the camp but had been repelled. Rumors spread that partisans had tried to liberate us. But another rumor says that an animal had simply triggered a mine. Whatever the case, I'm encouraged to think that maybe the Germans and Ukrainians feel far more vulnerable than they want us to believe.

A few weeks after this incident, we are again marched out from the barracks in the middle of the night. We are made to stand in the yard, surrounded by all the German personnel as well as the Ukrainian guards. Their guns are pointed at us, and I can see their fingers on the triggers. I hear shots coming from Camp 3. They are executing the prisoners there! I feel certain that next we will all be shot. As I fear, the Germans order the kapos to line us up. Then the kapos meticulously count and recount us. Everyone waits nervously to receive an order to march to Camp 3. But then, without any explanation, we are ordered back to the barracks. The following day a kapo tells us at roll call that, according to one of the Ukrainians, the prisoners in Camp 3 had dug a tunnel. They had been only a few yards from finishing it when they were caught. All of them have been executed. Apparently these prisoners may have hatched the same plot as the prisoners who had preceded them in Camp 3 several months earlier. In both instances the prisoners had died trying to escape.

The most hated kapo in the camp is the new chief kapo, named Berliner. Berliner's story is well known to everyone in the camp. He had been a normal prisoner like us, until he had one day been appointed to his current position. Everyone suspects that he has earned his position by betraying an escape plan developed by several kapos, including "Governor General" Mojsze. Each of these kapos had been killed just prior to Berliner's appointment. Since then he has revealed himself to us as a corrupt and brutal man, beating us without mercy on many occasions. But one night I am in the barracks when Berliner is called in by the other kapos. Then, in front of everyone, for all to see, they descend upon him. They quickly gag his mouth and begin beating him without mercy. It's clear from how the kapos are beating him—with repeated blows to the chest only—that they are trying to kill him without leaving marks. But even at about the age of fifty, Berliner is a stout and well-fed man whose body can absorb much punishment. The attack continues for several minutes. I take pleasure in each of Berliner's muffled screams. The beating ceases when someone sights Wagner entering the yard near the barracks. The kapos hurriedly whisk Berliner away to their room.

At the evening roll call, Kapo Pożycki reports that Berliner is ill. When Symcha and I return to the barracks, Pożycki takes Symcha aside and they speak together quietly. When Symcha returns, he tells me that Pożycki has asked him to prepare a poison that will finish off Berliner in the least detectable way possible. Symcha goes to the pharmacy to prepare a lethal dose of morphine, which he will hand over to Pożycki. The next morning Berliner's lifeless body is laid out in front of everyone, wrapped only in a blanket. Pożycki reports to the Germans that Berliner has died of a sudden illness. Frenzel orders that Berliner's body be burned immediately.

The morning after the killing, everyone wonders how the Germans will respond. Won't they suspect foul play? Surely the Germans know that the death of this hated kapo cannot be pure coincidence. They must surmise that the prisoners have taken revenge. Moreover, I fear that if they determine that Berliner has been poisoned, they will again suspect Symcha's involvement in securing the poison. But surprisingly there is no further investigation. Apparently the Germans have detested Kapo Berliner about as much as we have. A rumor spreads that Frenzel had indeed resented Berliner, perhaps because Berliner had foolishly acted outside the strict chain of command. Reportedly Frenzel had once ordered that all members of the Bahnhofkommando were entitled to an extra serving of food because they need to appear healthy to the incoming victims. But when Berliner became a kapo, he for some reason had decided to deny the additional food to the Bahnhofkommando. His newfound power had apparently affected his good judgment. This unilateral decision had probably cost Berliner his life. Frenzel would never have forgiven such a direct challenge to his authority by a Jew. The order to kill Berliner, if this story is true, had come from Frenzel himself.

If a kapo can be killed so easily, I ask myself, then why not a Ukrainian or even a German? I soon learn from Symcha that this thought has occurred to others as well: a small group of conspirators has already banded together with precisely those intentions. Because of my brother's access to poisons, he is invited to participate in the group. Though they are sworn to secrecy, one crisp evening in the beginning of October, Symcha takes me aside and tells me that he has attended several meetings of this group of conspirators. He says they are planning an escape from the camp in just two days from now.

"You must keep this a secret," Symcha tells me, "even from your friends." I give him my promise.

According to Symcha, the group is led by Leon "Lajbl" Feldhendler. Like everyone in the camp, I know and respect Leon. He is a rabbi's son from Żołkiewka, the same hometown as my heroic friend Mordechaj. Tall, handsome, well spoken, ethical, and—at about forty years of age—older than most of us in the camp, he is a fitting leader.

Symcha explains that forming an escape plan for a few people would be easy, but the conspirators' consciences will not allow it. They all know from past experience with the Germans that any prisoners left behind will suffer harsh reprisals. So, at Leon's behest, his group has established a goal of developing an escape plan for all six hundred prisoners in the camp. No one can be left behind. For months they have been searching for a way to carry out such a bold initiative, but without success; they have been unable to devise a plan that will free everyone.

Then a miracle had occurred. A little more than two weeks ago, on September 23, 1943, dozens of Soviet prisoners of war had arrived at Sobibór. I and everyone else in the camp had noticed them because they had still been wearing their Red Army uniforms when they marched into the camp. According to what Symcha has been told, the Germans had sent these men first to the Minsk Ghetto and then to Sobibór because these soldiers are all Jews. Because of the apparent need for heavy labor in a fourth subcamp of Sobibór, which has been under construction since the end of the summer, the Germans had selected about eighty people from these newcomers to help us. Symcha tells me that the conspirators have determined to make this decision a fatal mistake for the Germans.

Symcha says that prior to the arrival of the Soviet Jewish POWs, the critical weakness of Leon's group had been that it lacked members with military know-how. None of them had ever fought or killed before. But now they have exactly what they need: well-drilled, battle-tested Jewish soldiers who can plan and carry out a revolt with military precision. The leader of these Jewish POWs is a young lieutenant named Aleksandr "Sasha" Pechersky. Symcha tells me that soon after the arrival of the Soviets, Leon had approached Sasha. The two men had agreed to combine their strengths: Sasha and his men's military skills and Leon and his men's deep knowledge of the camp's operations. Together with less than a dozen coconspirators, they have begun in earnest to mastermind the revolt. The initial group of conspirators had intentionally been kept as small as possible, so that strict secrecy can be enforced. But the revolt is planned for just two days from now, so additional conspirators are being selectively recruited based on their abilities.

Symcha senses my excitement and appears very pleased by it. Now he has a question for me: "Do you want to help?"

"Of course!" I reply. "I will do anything to be involved."

"I thought so," says Symcha. "We are going to need messengers. I volunteered your services to the group, and they agreed to let you join. You will come with me to the meeting tonight so that you can meet everyone."

I am delighted. Symcha has one more thing to add: "You will need to keep this a complete secret. You can't tell any of your friends, not even Rosa." I again promise Symcha my secrecy.

In the evening Symcha brings me to a meeting in a corner of the women's barracks. About ten people are seated there, including Leon, Sasha, and a few of the other Soviet POWs. They are speaking to one another softly, but with intense concentration. Each man appears confident and determined.

I have already noticed these men in the previous days talking among themselves in small groups inside and outside the barracks. The planning must be quite active. There is also a beautiful woman prisoner from Germany seated next to Sasha. She appears to be his girlfriend, but Symcha informs me later that this is only a ploy. She has been enlisted so that Leon and Sasha will be able to exchange information with each other in the relative secrecy of the women's barracks. It is essential that Leon and Sasha not be seen alone with each other because a friendship between the respective elders of the Polish prisoners and the new military prisoners can provoke the unwanted attention of camp personnel and prisoners alike.

Symcha introduces me to the conspirators as his brother. Then Leon addresses me: "Fiszel, we will need people to carry messages. Are you prepared to help us?"

"I will do whatever I am assigned to do for the revolt," I answer, "and anything I can do to avenge the killing of my family and tens of thousands of women and children." Now I am crying. "Even if I die in the revolt, at least I will know that I have done something to fight the murderers."

"Good," Leon says. "And if you are caught or betrayed, are you prepared to die without telling the Germans the names of the people in this room or any of our secrets?"

I say that I am prepared.

"Then you are now one of us. Your job will be to relay messages. You will receive instructions on what you'll have to do. Remember, you must not tell anyone what we have spoken about."

I give Leon my word. Then Symcha speaks: "I think that Fiszel should begin taking as many jewels as possible from the sorting shed. We can then bury the jewels in the ground, so that they can be recovered after the war."

Leon lends his support to Symcha's idea. "Any of the prisoners who survive this war will be without possessions," the leader says. "We will be able to use these jewels to provide food and shelter for every former prisoner of Sobibór."

After the meeting Symcha also instructs me to take some jewels for ourselves. He says that he will conceal everything in medicine bottles. "We'll need them," says Symcha, "to pay people to hide us after the escape."

The next day I steal handfuls of jewels and coins from the sorting shed and put them in my pockets. I bring the jewels to the pharmacist's shop, where Symcha places most of them in a jar. We keep a few of the jewels in our pockets, as well as some paper money and a few gold and silver coins for our own immediate use if we really manage to escape. We cover the jar with a metal top and bring it back to the barracks. Then, in the dark of night, I bury the jar outside the barracks, a few feet below the sandy ground. Symcha tells me that the revolt is still planned for the next day, October 13. He says I am needed at the final planning session later in the evening. I cannot believe how quickly everything is moving.

At the meeting that night, Sasha and Leon brief me and several other boys on the entire plot and the role we will play in it. The escape plan, they say, consists of two phases. First, beginning at precisely 4:00 p.m., we will spend exactly one hour secretly eliminating key German officers, without visibly interrupting regular functions of the camp. For this phase we will capitalize on the greed and punctuality of the German officers. I and the other boys will be assigned to our normal jobs but will be on call to help lure the officers to their deaths. Upon receiving instructions from the leaders of the conspiracy, we may be asked to leave our posts, approach individual German officers, and tell them that we have found valuable items for them, such as leather coats and boots. We will then make appointments for the officers to go into the workshops in Camps 1 and 2 to try on these coats and boots. Once these officers arrive to pick up the promised goods, combat groups of three Jews in each shop will use axes and knives to kill each officer. The axes have been provided by carpenters, who routinely use them for their normal work. The knives have been stolen from the sorting shed as well as covertly fabricated by a goldsmith, Szlome Szmajzner, in the blacksmiths' workshop.

In addition to killing the German "brains" of the camp, the revolt's success will also hinge on stealing enough guns to fend off possible resistance from most of the hundred or so Ukrainian guards. Conspirators will acquire rifles and ammunition from the armory after killing the SS officer who guards it. And after each SS man is killed, the members of the responsible combat group will of course take the officer's pistol.

For everything to go smoothly and without detection, the conspirators have been forced to daringly enlist the kapos Pożycki and Bunio to assist with assigning conspirators to the workshops designated by Sasha. These kapos will also allow me and the other boys to communicate messages to and from Sasha during the critical first phase of the revolt.

The second phase will be even more dangerous than the first. It will entail the actual open revolt and escape of not just the conspirators but each and every prisoner in Sobibór except for those in Camp 3, whom we unfortunately have no way of contacting without jeopardizing the conspiracy. Just before the start of roll call at 5:00 p.m., a conspirator will cut the telephone wires and electricity lines. This will prevent German officers or Ukrainian guards from calling for reinforcements. Then Pożycki and Bunio will lead the prisoners in a march toward the front gate. Hopefully, the Ukrainian guards will not suspect any foul play because the presence of the kapos will make it appear to be a work detail. Then the leaders of the revolt will announce to everyone that they have killed the camp's leaders, and they will direct everyone to walk to freedom through the front gate. Knowing that some Ukrainian guards have deserted the German cause in the past, if they do not open the front gate then the Soviet POWs will also call out in Russian to the guards that the Red Army is closing in and the Germans are losing the war. They will implore the Ukrainians to lay down their arms, allow us through the front gate, and join us in defeating the Germans. If the plan works, every prisoner will be able to march to freedom through the camp's front gate. If not, we will need to escape through the fences and the minefield that surrounds the camp. There are no other options. In any case, night will soon descend. Whoever can make it to the forest will be able to rely on the hours of darkness to gain a head start on any remaining Germans or Ukrainians who might pursue us through the woods.

This is the plan, but if anything goes wrong, we are told that it will be every man for himself. If the secret killings are discovered by the Germans before the conspirators can carry out the plan to completion, we will continue with the mass revolt, but it will come down to a shoot-out between us and the Ukrainians guards and the remaining Germans. The conspirators will have use of as many guns as they can possibly take from the murdered

SS men and the armory. They will hopefully also be able to utilize ammunition stolen by several women conspirators who work in the German quarters.

Everyone agrees to the plan.

When we leave the meeting, Symcha tells me: "There is even more good news. The camp commander has been away on leave for the past few days. So has Gomerski. But today Wagner also left!" Several conspirators have seen Wagner departing in a car with some of his belongings. He has apparently left the camp to take vacation. If this is true, then our chances of successfully escaping have improved dramatically. Wagner is both the fiercest and the most intuitive of all the SS officers. Every conspirator has naturally worried that Wagner would sniff out the revolt during its first phase, when he would be able to see conspirators entering buildings that they do not customarily enter. And even if Wagner somehow did not sense what was wrong, he would be the most difficult of all of the SS men to kill. Even with more than one man assigned to kill him, the muscular Wagner might put up a formidable fight, especially if he somehow managed to survive the first blows of the axes. Now, without him in the camp, there is much to be grateful for.

Symcha then says that we must prepare for the "every-man-for-himself" scenario. In such a situation, chaos will ensue. He says that we should try to stay together, but if we become separated, we must prepare for the challenge of finding each other in the dense forest. Symcha proposes code words that we can call out to locate each other. His word will be "Wagner," and mine will be "Frenzel." I understand the logic of using the two German officers' names. If we escape the camp, we will likely be hunted by any surviving German or Ukrainian; by calling out the two German officers' names, we will draw less attention to ourselves than if we use other words. And there is no chance that we will ever forget these names.

Symcha also hands me a compass and tells me that if I can't find him in the forest, I should use the compass to guide me back to Izbica, where we should look for each other in an area of the cemetery where we can hopefully hide. And in the event that I am injured by mines or bullets, he tells me to use the morphine he once gave me to die in peace, because we have heard rumors that people caught escaping in the past have been burned alive by the Germans. He says he has also prepared similarly lethal doses of morphine for the other conspirators.

Finally, Symcha informs me of the role he will play during the uprising. He will saw wood outside the workshops where the killings are planned. The killings must be carried out as quietly as possible. Any audible cries from the SS officers can alert others and compromise the conspirators' ability to kill the remaining officers. So if Symcha hears any German officer crying out, he and the men with him will bang their tools to muffle the sounds.

I know we can count on the Soviet soldiers to carry out their assignments. But what about the other prisoners? They aren't soldiers. They have no training or experience in killing. "Do you think the Polish Jews will be able to kill the Germans," I ask, "when they have never killed before?"

"We'll rely on the Soviets as much as possible," Symcha answers. "But some of us will also be asked to carry out the killings. No one will be scared. Killing is the only choice we have."

Symcha is right. Despite the danger I even wish that I could be one of the members of the killing squads.

Until now I have kept the plot a secret from Rosa. Though Symcha says it is imperative that I keep this information to myself, I now must tell her. Rosa needs to be prepared for what is going to happen. So I find her in the women's barracks and bring her outside to a place where nobody can hear us. Then I quietly tell her: "I am going to reveal something to you that I am not supposed to. If you tell anybody this secret, we could all be killed. We are going to revolt tomorrow. My brother and I have been involved as part of the planning group. I might carry messages during the revolt, but then we will all escape together. After the roll call, every prisoner in Camps 1 and 2 will run out of Sobibór and into the forest. Because I love you and I want to be with you, I want to tell you so that we can hold hands and run beside each other. Who knows how long we'll have to remain in the forest? But try to wear warm clothing under your normal clothes. In case we get separated, we'll look for each other in the woods. And in case you get injured, take the bottle of morphine with you."

Rosa turns pale. She says that she is scared. "The Germans are not invincible," I say. "The Soviet soldiers tell us that their comrades are beating back the Germans and that the front is very close. But we can't wait for the Soviets to liberate us. The Germans will kill us if the Soviets get close."

Rosa knows I am right, but it does not appear to diminish her fear. "I know it is dangerous, but we must do this," I continue. "We can take vengeance. And maybe somebody can get out and tell the world what is happening here."

Now Rosa is sobbing. "What if we die?" she says.

"We will die if we do nothing," I say. "All of us agree that it will be better to die by bullets than by gas and take vengeance for our dead families."

"But I am still scared of dying!" she cries.

"If you are scared, it is good," I say. "It means that you still want to live, and that is what you will need to escape. Don't worry; I will run with you. We'll make it out of here together. Now promise me that you will not tell anyone about this."

She promises. "Don't worry," I say. "Symcha and I even have a plan for what to do once we reach the forest. We'll have money and a compass that will take us back to Izbica, where hopefully we can hide until the Soviets come."

Rosa says we might have more luck hiding with a business acquaintance of her father not far from Sobibór. "Maybe," I say. "But at least I know the terrain in and around Izbica. Let's decide where to go when we get to the forest."

Rosa has one more request: "Fiszel, if I die and you survive, you should go back to my family's house and recover the jewels that my family hid in our house. They are behind the wallboards of our attic."

"OK," I say. "But we are going to return to your home together. You'll see."

Rosa gives me their address and tells me exactly which wallboard contains the hidden items. I am still carrying a cache of my own: the handful of jewels, coins, and paper money that I have stolen earlier in the day. Before we part for the night, Rosa returns to her barracks and sews these valuables into our clothing.

Before going to sleep, Symcha and I recite the kaddish for our parents. We also pray silently for the success of the revolt tomorrow.

10

Escape from Sobibór

The day arrives cloudy and cold. I have never been so nervous or excited in all of my seventeen years. This may be the last day of my life and the end of my suffering. Or I will live. Only two things are certain: today we will take vengeance, and everything will change. I eat breakfast and go to work in the sorting shed as usual. I begin counting the hours until the revolt will begin. At around 10:30 a.m., however, my heart sinks: I spot dozens of German soldiers arriving in trucks! Much as I want to deny it, I know that in all probability there is only one reason why the Germans would call in reinforcements, and that is to help with killing all the prisoners. Perhaps the Germans have found out about our escape plot. Or they have decided to close the camp, and they expect us to resist the liquidation. In either case we can never stage the revolt in the presence of so much extra manpower. I can't believe that we have come so close only to be so disappointed in the end. What if we had been able to stage the revolt just one day earlier? Then maybe we could have made it out alive! As I work in the sorting shed, I receive a message from another conspirator: "Postponed, pass it on."

I try not to worry. I remind myself that we don't know for certain why the German soldiers are here. And Leon and Sasha have only "postponed," not canceled, the revolt. After the evening roll call, however, my hopes revive. Prisoners spread the news that they have seen the troops drinking together and carousing with women. More importantly, the soldiers have already left the camp. It appears that the German soldiers have merely come to Sobibór for some socializing. Symcha tells me the good news: the revolt will take place tomorrow, October 14.

One of Judaism's most important festivals, Sukkot, has already begun at sundown and will continue into tomorrow.[1] But regardless of the need for the most religious Jews among us to observe the holiday, the rabbi's son, Leon, must have agreed with Sasha that the revolt cannot wait any longer. We fear that, any day now, the Germans will suddenly kill everyone in the camp. Delaying even one more day will risk everyone's lives. Having always wanted to be a doctor, I know what Leon knows: that the obligation to save lives takes precedence over observance of holidays.[2] Furthermore, the risk of the conspiracy being compromised has increased greatly now that so many people have been let in on the secret. The group of conspirators has also heard that Wagner is due back from vacation the day after tomorrow, on October 15.

I inform Rosa of what has transpired. I still have hope and confidence that we will succeed, but deep inside I wonder if this will be the last night of our lives together. After spending the entire evening in the women's barracks with Rosa, I tell her how much I love her and kiss her goodnight. I pray it will not be our final kiss.

Back in the men's barracks, I take a long time to fall asleep. I am overflowing with excitement, looking forward to finally taking vengeance and escaping. But knowing that this might also be the last time I ever lie down to sleep, I also allow myself to look back on my life. Could I have done anything differently to escape my fate? Would I have never ended up in these barracks if I had somehow fled to Palestine before the war or accompanied Jakub to the Soviet Union during the war's early days? No, I cannot blame myself—I had done everything I could do to save my life and my family members' lives. Then I become terribly sad thinking of all the things I still want to do: marry Rosa, have children with her, and live a happy, productive life in Palestine. All of this could have been, and none of this will be. I should accept that I may die without knowing the joys of standing under the marriage canopy, raising children, and seeing the Holy Land. But I refuse to despair. As I have learned how to do from my most impoverished neighbors in Izbica, I stay optimistic by thanking God for the many gifts with which I have been blessed in my short life.

In the morning the weather is again dark and gray, but I am happier than ever. I am assigned as usual to work in the sorting shed in Camp 2.

Again I begin to count the hours until 4:00 p.m. At lunch I can feel the nervous excitement among the conspirators as well as many of their friends. Clearly I am not the only one who has let the secret slip.

As the day continues, I can barely concentrate on my work. Finally, just after 4:00 p.m., from my vantage point I see SS Unterscharführer Josef Wolf being approached by a teenage boy who, like me, is one of the on-call messengers. According to plan the boy appears to tell Wolf that a very expensive coat has been found for him and that he is welcome to try it on for fit. Wolf nods in approval and walks away in the direction of the storeroom. From what Symcha has told me, I know this is one of the locations where an ambush awaits!

I am incredibly anxious to know if the conspirators in the storeroom have succeeded. After a few minutes, I cannot stand to wait any longer. I need to know Wolf's fate. Have we really killed him? I go to the storeroom to see if I can find out what has happened. As I walk past, I glance inside as casually as possible. Wolf is on the ground, dead and covered in blood. Two of the Soviet POWs are dragging him behind the piles of clothes to hide him. A rush of happiness runs through my body. I say to myself: This is for my sisters and my niece and all the Jews who have died in the gas chambers. Whatever happens, I at least have some satisfaction in knowing that we have taken vengeance.

Now that we have taken the life of a German officer, there is no turning back. The revolt is happening right now! I know that other killings must have already taken place in Camp 1 and more are planned in Camp 2. At about 4:50 p.m., fifty minutes after the revolt had begun and ten minutes before the usual time for roll call, the bugle sounds, calling everyone to the main yard.

People begin to assemble. As I look around, it is obvious that now even more people know about the revolt. Many appear optimistic and are quietly wishing one another luck. Some prisoners have even prepared for life in the forest by dressing in warmer clothing than usual. I quickly find Rosa and Symcha so that we can be ready to escape together. Symcha says that we have succeeded in killing as many as eleven German officers. Several Ukrainian guards have also been killed when the opportunity arose. A few officers, however, have escaped our grasp by not showing up for their appointments. Wishing to avoid detection by these remaining officers, Leon and Sasha have ordered Kapo Pożycki to tell the bugle boy to sound the bugle for a general roll call a few minutes early, so that everyone can gather and the escape can proceed as soon as possible.

As people steadily arrive, it becomes even more evident that the escape is about to begin. A few people have brought sacks of provisions and warm clothing to the roll call. Some are visibly happy, and others appear nervous. We really should not wait any longer or it will be too obvious to the remaining Germans and Ukrainians that something is amiss. Now almost everyone has arrived.

We hear shouts from another area of the camp, followed quickly by distant gunshots and more shouts.

Something must have gone wrong. None of the conspirators would have used guns before the start of the actual open revolt. The few remaining Germans or some of the Ukrainian guards have probably discovered the plot and are now fighting back somewhere else in the camp. In only a few moments the fight can reach our area.

Leon and Sasha realize what must be done. Immediately they jump on top of a table at the front of the yard and call out to everyone:

"Brothers! The moment of destiny has come. Most of the Germans have been killed. Let us rise and destroy this place. We have little chance of surviving, but at least we will die fighting with honor. If anyone survives, bear witness to what happened here! Tell the world about this place!"

I quickly promise myself that, yes, if I survive the next moments, I will fulfill Leon and Sasha's wishes; I will tell everyone beyond this forest about this cursed place and its brave prisoners.

Chaos takes over. A large group of shouting prisoners rushes toward the main gate. Some of the conspirators begin to set fire to a few of the camp's buildings. Others are storming the armory in a bid to acquire weapons. Ukrainian guards are shooting at us from the watchtowers. The main gate is well covered by these Ukrainians and now obstructed by the bodies of the first group of prisoners mowed down by the machine guns. Frenzel, whom we have not been able to lure to his death, emerges from his quarters and begins firing at close range on the people massed by the main gate. He is killing dozens of people.

While running and ducking for cover, people seek an escape route other than the main gate. Some are shooting back at the Germans and Ukrainians with the few pistols and machine guns that we have managed to obtain from the officers we killed. Nearly everyone begins scattering in the direction of the triple row of ten-feet-high barbed-wire fences that separates us from the minefields and the forest. A few people remain in the yard, paralyzed by indecision. Because the revolt has been kept secret from them, maybe they assume that the war is over and that they are safer remaining in the camp than fleeing through machine-gun fire and minefields. Or maybe they are placing their lives in God's hands. Even Leon cannot convince them to run. Some of them sit motionless. Others stand and pray.

But most people are now doing whatever they can to get past the barbed wire. Some are climbing over the fences; some are crawling under them. Others are hacking away at the barbed wire with axes. Some are even trying to scale the fences using ladders that the conspirators have prepared for this scenario. The ladders are collapsing under the weight of the people, but bringing down the fences along with them. Many of these first people to cross the fences are immediately killed by mine explosions.

With the sounds of bullets and detonating mines surrounding us, I know that we cannot wait much longer to make our mad dash from the camp. Now that the option of escaping through the main gate no longer exists, I know we have no choice other than to traverse the minefield. But first we must overcome the barbed-wire fences. I quickly scan for the safest and most vulnerable area.

"Look at that part of the fence," I yell to Symcha and Rosa, pointing to a section of the fence near the Germans' quarters. Here there are only two rows of fences, and both have already been cut down by conspirators or trampled by the escaping masses.

"OK," Symcha says. "Let's run for it. Follow me!"

I grab Rosa's hand and together we all dart toward the area to which I have pointed. Although the fences have collapsed, barbed wire still juts up from the ground to a height of about five feet. I let go of Rosa so that I can brush one of the wires aside with my hands. One of my fingers is immediately cut by the barbs and begins to bleed all over my hand. But I barely notice.

As soon as I get past the wires, I reach behind me so that Rosa can again take my hand. But she does not take it. I turn around and discover that she is no longer behind me. Symcha is also gone. I look in despair in all directions for both of them. I can't see them anywhere.

We have become separated.

I call out through the clatter of the machine guns, "Rosa! Rosa! Symcha! Symcha!" But there is no answer. A hundred thoughts race through my mind. Maybe Rosa and Symcha have been pushed to a different section of the fence by the onrushing masses. I can only pray they have not been shot. I might be the last member of my family left alive. But I cannot think that way. Stay focused on getting out of this cursed place, I tell myself. There are only a few critical decisions to make. Should I wait for the machine-gun fire to die down? Or should I make a run for it now? And in which direction should I run?

Dozens of people around me begin to steadily get past the tangle of wires. I crouch down to take cover from the bullets while considering what to do next. People start to run past me and into the minefield. Calling out one last time to Rosa and Symcha, I see mines exploding just a few feet away. Many prisoners lie motionless in front of me, felled by the mines just a few hundred yards from the freedom of the forest. My ears are ringing.

The minefield seems to be the only available path. But judging from the fates of those who have gone before me, death seems virtually assured if I try to enter the fields. I quickly consider whether there are less perilous options. A thought occurs to me: it might be safer to begin my run from directly in front of the officers' quarters. Perhaps the Germans have attempted to protect their quarters from damage by not placing mines nearby.

So I make my way over to the area of the fence that runs past the Germans' quarters. I visualize running, as light on my feet as I can, in a direct line from the buildings to the forest. From this part of the camp, I will need to traverse a distance of about fifteen hundred feet to reach the forest. I begin my careful sprint across the minefield, crouching down as much as I can, with the sound of bullets flying all around me. I run past dozens of people who have been felled by mines or bullets, some of them not yet dead but too injured to move. They have all helped clear a path for me through the minefield.

After about thirty seconds of running, I am more than halfway to the forest. My plan seems to be working.

I take another few steps and feel a strange sensation beneath my feet. Next comes an explosion.

I am thrown about five feet into the air by the detonation of a mine. I land on my back.

I ask myself if I am still alive.

I look at my arms. They are still there. I touch my legs. They are still attached, too. I try to stand up. I do so. Apparently I have only stepped on a dummy mine. It must have been an air mine meant to alert the Germans to any saboteurs or escapees without damaging the nearby buildings. My intuition has proved correct.

I continue running. I recognize one of the people lying on the ground. He is my friend Josel Siegel, a boy about my age from Siedliszcze who has worked with me in the sorting shed. He is bleeding profusely. He is so close to the freedom beyond Sobibór that I must at least try to help him. I run over to him and attempt to bring him to his feet. As I try to lift him, I see that his eyes are closed. I yell to him, "Get up! We are free!" The sounds of machine-gun fire and bullets surround us. Moreover, it quickly becomes clear that I don't have the strength to carry him far. If I try dragging him to the forest, we will likely both be killed by the machine guns. I must make the best decision for both him and me. I think of what I would choose if I were in Josel's place.

I leave Josel behind.

Only a few more yards separate me from the forest. The dead and the dying are still all around me. The smoky air smells of gunpowder. But with each step closer to the forest, my heart begins to sing. In those final few moments, not once do I look back.

I enter the forest. I am free.

Other prisoners are circulating through the woods, unsure of which direction to go. I scan their faces, but none belongs to Symcha or Rosa. It is clear that at least dozens and probably hundreds have escaped. I decide to keep running as far away as possible from the sounds of the gunfire. I am concentrating on getting around the trees when I step into a dark puddle of water. My feet immediately get stuck in mud. My whole body begins to sink. The swampy water begins to rise up to my waist. I begin to panic. But I quickly compose myself and use all my strength to lift my feet and body out.

I continue running for about one hundred more yards, covered in mud. Then I hear Symcha's voice. He has found me among the trees. "Fiszel, are you OK? Are you OK? Are you injured?"

We hug each other. My brother is alive, and we have escaped Sobibór together! We haven't even needed to use our passwords.

But Symcha is alone.

"Where is Rosa?" I ask.

"I don't know," Symcha says. "I tried to stay with her, but we got separated. Don't worry; we'll find her."

But I am greatly worried. Rosa is young and strong, but those qualities might not have been enough to get her safely through the bullets and mines. And even if she is somewhere in this forest, she will need help to survive.

We agree that we need to begin putting as much distance as possible between us and Sobibór. We consult our compasses and try to run in a southwest direction, toward Izbica, where at least our knowledge of the terrain might give us a better chance of surviving. As we run, I look around as much as I can for signs of Rosa. After just a few minutes of running, we happen upon one of my friends from the camp, Jankiel. I ask if he has seen Rosa. He says he has. "What direction did she go?" I ask.

Jankiel says that he had been running near her, through the minefields, when a mine exploded directly beneath her. "The explosion threw her into the air. She landed right next to me," he says. "I saw her die."

I begin to cry uncontrollably. But only for a few seconds. We must keep running. There is no time to spare.

It is not at all easy to traverse the terrain in which we find ourselves. The forest is thick with trees. The ground is wet and swampy in many places. Nevertheless, everyone is running as fast as he or she can. Groups are forming spontaneously. As we begin running with Jankiel, several of his friends run by and tell him to come with them. He leaves. Then a friend of Symcha's from the camp, Aaron Licht, appears with two other escapees, Josel Licht and another man named Begleter. Symcha stops for a moment to talk with Aaron. I hear them discussing where to go. After just a few moments, Symcha turns to me and says that we should go with Aaron's group. I am still too upset about Rosa to be of any help in deciding our next steps. I tell Symcha that I'll do whatever he thinks is best.

By now it is dark. Flares light up the sky. The Germans are searching for us intensely. Although to them we are still lowly Jews, we are also eye-witnesses who can reveal to the world the atrocities that we have seen. We must keep fleeing from the area of Sobibór. We run and walk through the forest throughout the night, as fast as we can, in the direction of the village of Oszczyce, where Aaron has a Catholic business acquaintance whom he thinks he can trust to hide us in exchange for money. Between the five of us, we have several items to help us survive: compasses, jewels, money, food, a few small guns, some ammunition, and a grenade that one of the Soviet soldiers gave to Symcha. Besides the swamps, many areas also have deep ditches a few hundred yards in length that have apparently been dug to defend against tanks. We are constantly forced to run around these ditches. But thanks to our compasses, we are able to maintain our direction and not run around in circles.

When morning arrives, we decide it will be too dangerous to push on in the light of day. So we hide in the densest thicket we can find near the road from Sobibór to Chełm. Utterly exhausted, we eat what little food that we have managed to bring with us from the camp. We then quickly fall asleep. A few hours later we are awakened by the sound of sirens. Fear quickly turns to relief when we discover that the sirens are simply ambulances. And when we then surmise the purpose of these ambulances—that they must be carrying the dead SS officers to Chełm—we five grown men hug one another with unrestrained joy. It is the first moment that we have taken to truly celebrate our accomplishment. Not only have we escaped from Sobibór—we have taken vengeance![3]

Poland under German occupation.

Symcha (*back row, far left*) and Jakub (*back row, second from right*) with their Zionist youth group before the war. Photo in author's private collection.

Jakub (*at top*) with his Zionist youth group before the war. Photo in author's private collection.

My sister Brancha. Photo in author's private collection.

My family in 1940. *Back row, from left*: Rywka's mother-in-law and father-in-law, Symcha, me, Rywka; *front row, from left*: Toba, my mother holding Sara, my father holding Yosel, Brancha. Photo in author's private collection.

Top, from left: Emil and Erna Rosenberger, in portraits from their "Jewish identification cards" issued by Nazi Germany, 1938. Reproduced by permission of Stadtarchiv Karlsruhe, 1/AEST 1239. *Bottom, from left*: Ilse and Herta Rosenberger, passport application portraits for passage to the Netherlands, 1938. Reproduced by permission of Landesarchivs Baden-Württemberg, 330 nos. 1009, 1010.

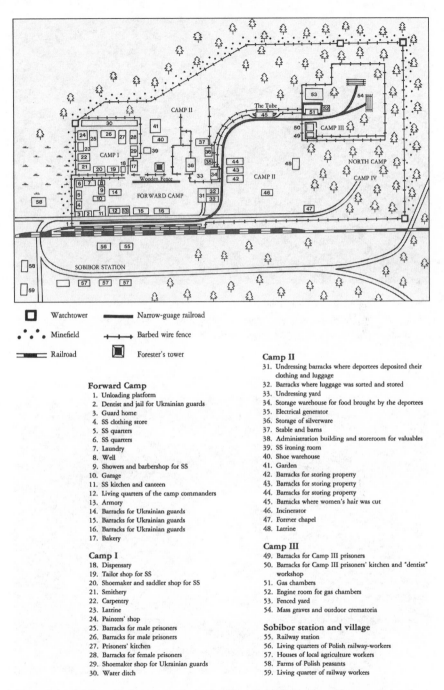

☐	Watchtower
•∴•	Minefield
▰▰	Railroad
▬▬	Narrow-guage railroad
+—+—→	Barbed wire fence
▣	Forester's tower

Forward Camp
1. Unloading platform
2. Dentist and jail for Ukrainian guards
3. Guard home
4. SS clothing store
5. SS quarters
6. SS quarters
7. Laundry
8. Well
9. Showers and barbershop for SS
10. Garage
11. SS kitchen and canteen
12. Living quarters of the camp commanders
13. Armory
14. Barracks for Ukrainian guards
15. Barracks for Ukrainian guards
16. Barracks for Ukrainian guards
17. Bakery

Camp I
18. Dispensary
19. Tailor shop for SS
20. Shoemaker and saddler shop for SS
21. Smithery
22. Carpentry
23. Latrine
24. Painters' shop
25. Barracks for male prisoners
26. Barracks for male prisoners
27. Prisoners' kitchen
28. Barracks for female prisoners
29. Shoemaker shop for Ukrainian guards
30. Water ditch

Camp II
31. Undressing barracks where deportees deposited their clothing and luggage
32. Barracks where luggage was sorted and stored
33. Undressing yard
34. Storage warehouse for food brought by the deportees
35. Electrical generator
36. Storage of silverware
37. Stable and barns
38. Administration building and storeroom for valuables
39. SS ironing room
40. Shoe warehouse
41. Garden
42. Barracks for storing property
43. Barracks for storing property
44. Barracks for storing property
45. Barracks where women's hair was cut
46. Incinerator
47. Former chapel
48. Latrine

Camp III
49. Barracks for Camp III prisoners
50. Barracks for Camp III prisoners' kitchen and "dentist" workshop
51. Gas chambers
52. Engine room for gas chambers
53. Fenced yard
54. Mass graves and outdoor crematoria

Sobibor station and village
55. Railway station
56. Living quarters of Polish railway-workers
57. Houses of local agriculture workers
58. Farms of Polish peasants
59. Living quarter of railway workers

Map of the Sobibór death camp as drawn by Alisa Gold. Reproduced by permission from *The Pictorial History of the Holocaust*, ed. Yitzhak Arad and Yad Vashem (Jerusalem: Yad Vashem Publications, 1990), 294. © 1990 by Yad Vashem and Yitzhak Arad.

Railway station at the Sobibór death camp. Reproduced by permission from *The Pictorial History of the Holocaust*, ed. Yitzhak Arad and Yad Vashem (Jerusalem: Yad Vashem Publications, 1990), 294. © 1990 by Yad Vashem and Yitzhak Arad.

A party of Sobibór camp staff at the Swallow's Nest. Gustav Wagner is seated at top right. Reproduced by permission of Yad Vashem. © Yad Vashem, Jerusalem.

Clockwise from top left: Karl Frenzel, Hubert Gomerski, and Sasha Pechersky. Reproduced by permission of Yad Vashem. © Yad Vashem.

Above: Joining several other Sobibór escapees, including Josef Herszman (*second from left*) and Meier Ziss (*second from right*), in Lublin, 1944. The gun on the table was stolen from an SS officer during the Sobibór revolt. Photo in author's private collection. *Left*: Maria, Michał, and Jan Mazurek. Reproduced by permission of Beata Wójcik and Janusz Mazurek.

Me, Lola, and Symcha in Zamość, 1945. Photo in author's private collection.

Me, Jakub, Lola, and Symcha in Zamość, 1945. Photo in author's private collection.

Jakub and Ada. Photo in author's private collection.

Apprenticing as a dentist in the American zone of occupation in postwar Germany. Photo in author's private collection.

A political demonstration at the Heidenheim DP camp, ca. 1947. Mala stands in the center of the front row beneath a Yiddish sign that urges "liquidation" of the DP camps. Photo in author's private collection.

Visiting the area of the Jewish cemetery, ca. 2000, in Izbica where my mother was shot and buried in a mass grave. Bullet holes are visible near the top of the gravestone. Photo in author's private collection.

Standing alongside Maria Mazurek and her family in Tarzymiechy in 2000, in front of the place where she hid me beneath her family's barn during the war. Photo in author's private collection.

After leading a tour of Sobibór for Polish children, 2000. Photo in author's private collection.

With my brother Symcha in front of the mound of human ashes in Sobibór's former Camp 3, 2008. Photo in author's private collection.

Leading a documentary film crew through the neighborhood where I grew up in Izbica, 2008. Photo in author's private collection.

In front of the building that served as the wartime headquarters of the Gestapo in Izbica, 2008. Photo in author's private collection.

The train tracks next to the old movie house in Izbica, 2008. Photo in author's private collection.

With Joseph in 2010. Photo in author's private collection.

My children in 1985. *From left*: Michael, Evelyn, Simone, Jeffrey, and Joseph. Photo in author's private collection.

My eleven eldest grandchildren. Photos in author's private collection.

11

New Dangers

In the evening we gather some sugar beets from the fields to eat, and then take off through the woods. After about three hours of walking, we encounter a group of ten ragtag Polish partisans, two of whom are women. The group is armed with guns and ammunition. Right away we know this can be a very delicate situation. They can help us live, but they can also kill us because of whatever money and valuables they surely suspect we are hiding. And if they are independence fighters who are against both German *and* Soviet occupation of Poland, then they will have even more motivation to kill us because they might hold the misperception that all Jews are Communists.

We decide to act as friendly as possible toward the partisans. To prove our credentials, we tell them that we have killed the Germans at Sobibór and want "to continue to fight the German swine until Poland is once again free." They confer among themselves before inviting us to join them. Who knows what they are really thinking? Maybe they just need more time to decide how best to rob and kill us cleanly, without the gunfire that can call attention to their location. But we don't have anywhere to run. We must live in the forest until we can find a better alternative, and these partisans offer us our best chance of surviving this harsh and alien environment.

For food we can depend on the partisan women to cook whatever we can procure from nearby farmers. We sleep in wood-covered pits, where we are able to make concealed fires to keep us warm. The partisans teach us to shoot guns and lay mines. Soon we are partisans ourselves, venturing out on our first mission to place mines on railroad tracks. Despite the danger of the work, it is quite satisfying to know that we are helping to defeat the

Germans. But it becomes clearer every day that our presence irritates some of the partisans. Several of them refuse to work with us entirely, standing to the side and never helping us at all. Their resentment becomes most evident when, one night, we overhear them talking with one another: "They are Jews. They don't belong with us."

Despite the fact that we are not welcome, several weeks go by without any problems. We even venture into a small town and have photographs taken of each of us. I treasure my photo because, as far as I know, all the other photos taken of me previously may have been destroyed by now. I still do not know if I will live until the end of the war. But if I am to die, this photo will tell the world that I existed. People will see what my face looked like. And they will know that despite being sent to Sobibór, I have survived until this day.

One day the partisans ask us to bring them to our home cities to recover valuables. We lie, claiming that we have not left anything hidden in these places. They ask if we have any relatives who have hid valuables in other towns. We tell them that all our relatives are very poor and have probably died already. The partisans finally relent, but we can sense that they are increasingly unhappy with us. What use are we really to them? That night they send us out on a mission to place mines on a railroad track. We think about making a run for it whenever we reach a safe distance from them. But they make the decision for us: as we walk toward the tracks, the partisans begin firing their guns directly at our backs. We run for our lives.

Despite the darkness and the thick forest, we do our best to flee as far away as we can. By morning we have made it to the home of Aaron's business acquaintance in the village of Oszczyce, only a few miles from Izbica. Aaron approaches the home while we hide in the nearby woods. An hour later he returns to say that he has struck a deal. Aaron has agreed to pay the man on a weekly basis, in return for food and shelter. We all chip in some of the gold and silver that we have, being careful to retain enough to get us by over the next few uncertain months. Aaron leads us to the barn that will be our home.

The barn is a two-story structure containing straw and the farmer's few cows and chickens. We construct a double wall of straw on the top floor of the barn and hide there during the day. The farmer's wife brings us our first meal and promises to do so every day. Even though her husband is demanding payment from us, the generous portions of food she provides along with the kindest of smiles tell us that she genuinely cares for our welfare. Within a few days, we are feeling healthy enough to go outside at night to exercise and stretch for a couple of hours.

Everything goes smoothly for about two months. We pay the man, his wife cooks for us, and we exercise. I even have time to think about how lucky I am to be alive and to have seen the Nazi murderers killed. I allow myself to look forward to a better future, whenever this war ends, which we expect to come soon.

One day the woman who cares for us comes running to the barn, holding an empty pail used to milk the cows, yelling, "My children, save yourselves! Run! Run while you can!"

In the distance we discern a pack of civilians with guns running toward the house. Clearly someone has betrayed us. The likeliest culprit is Aaron's friend himself. We heard him coming home drunk from town on many of the last few nights. This conduct could have easily aroused the townspeople's suspicions. Here is a formerly modest man who is now throwing money around, apparently buying as much vodka as he can drink. The townspeople have surely suspected that his newfound riches come from hiding Jews—perhaps they have even managed to force a confession from him—and now they are going to set things right. We assume that this means robbing and killing us.

There is nothing we can do but flee as fast as we can. We jump as if by parachute from the top of the barn down to the ground behind it. Luckily the crops in the nearby fields are very high, so they both cushion our falls and prevent the search group from seeing us. After we've put a few miles between the house and ourselves, we begin walking and trying to figure out where to go next.

When Symcha and I were last in Izbica, we had known that a Jewish friend of Symcha, a man named Duczy, had been living openly without any problems in the village of Tarzymiechy, just a few miles south of Izbica. He had been born and raised in Tarzymiechy and had always been on good terms with the Poles there. He had been so well liked that he had lived there safely, without fear of being betrayed to the Germans. Symcha had also heard that Duczy had successfully arranged for several Jews to hide on the farm of a Catholic family in the village. Without any other decent options, Symcha and I decide to try our luck. Aaron Licht agrees to join us. Josel Licht and Begleter, however, decide to venture out on their own, believing it will be safer to travel and hide in a smaller group.

We arrive in Tarzymiechy before daybreak and quickly find Duczy's house. He immediately offers to help us. Because Symcha is a pharmacist, Duczy arranges for us to hide at the home of a man whose wife suffers from diabetes. Symcha will be able to provide insulin injections to the man's wife. Under cover of night, Duczy brings us to the home, and we are given a place to sleep in their barn. Symcha begins administering daily injections to the man's wife. Her condition gradually improves. We hope the family will remain dependent on us and will continue to shelter us. However, we feel that this situation is still not as safe as possible. If the infirm wife falls ill or dies, we will no longer be needed. So we ask Duczy to find a different place for us to hide. The next day he arrives with news that he has arranged for us to hide at a small farm where the Mazurek family lives.

Duczy tells us that Michał Mazurek is a middle-aged farmer with a wife, a daughter, and three sons. He says Mr. Mazurek seems like a man we can trust. On the other hand, with our lives at stake, we cannot risk trusting anyone completely. In these desperate times, anyone—even an upright farmer whom our friend trusts—can be tempted to rob and kill us. This creates an immediate dilemma. We must pay Mr. Mazurek for the food he will provide to us and the risk he is taking by hiding us—we know that anyone can be killed if he or she is caught hiding Jews—but we do not want Mr. Mazurek to know that we are carrying so many valuables. Symcha develops a clever solution. Upon meeting Mr. Mazurek, Symcha presents him with just a small amount of our jewels as payment for the food and shelter that he will provide. Symcha and Mr. Mazurek agree that this will cover our first month's stay. For future payments Symcha says that he is owed money by several business acquaintances in Izbica and that he can secretly walk the short distance to Izbica each month to pick up some of the money he is owed and return with it. In reality Symcha is not owed money by anyone in Izbica; he simply plans to act as if he is sneaking away to Izbica one night each month. He will hide overnight in the fields, then return to pay Mr. Mazurek in the morning with a portion of the money and jewels that we already have in our possession. Mr. Mazurek seems satisfied, and an agreement is reached.

The arrangement with Mr. Mazurek turns out to be much better than we ever expected. He has a small farm of a few acres that can sustain his family and us. We dig a pit in their barn in which we hide during the daytime. We cover the pit with as much hay as possible. Mr. Mazurek's wife, Maria, and their teenaged daughter, Stefka, are both extremely kind. Using milk pails, they deliver hearty meals to us every day and also remove our pails of human waste whenever necessary. The system works well because to the neighbors it appears that the Mazureks are merely carrying the buckets to and from the barn to milk their cow.

Yet we still have reason to worry. Any of the Mazurek family's six members can decide our fate. We are entrusting our lives to each of these six people. This means that we are vulnerable on six different fronts. Our greatest concerns are Mr. Mazurek's sons. His youngest son, Jan, is only eight years old. Surely his parents have ordered him not to breathe a word about us to his friends. But is this young boy mature enough to keep his family's secret safe? If he tells even just one friend about us, that friend can tell his parents and they might then come to rob and kill us. Furthermore, we soon learn that Mr. Mazurek's oldest sons, Józef and Stanislaw, are members of the local Armia Krajowa (AK) resistance movement.[1] Based on our prior experience with the partisans in the forest, we are fearful that we might be betrayed again. But we have nowhere else to go, and we judge that as long as we continue to pay for our stay, none of the sons will turn on us. Most of all, however, we feel secure in knowing that the sons will not risk their parents' lives by betraying them to the Germans.

After a few weeks, Duczy decides that our situation is so promising that he can hide another Jew with us. So one day he brings Lola Pelc, a woman in her late thirties who is a member of the Pelc family that Symcha and I were close with in Izbica. She has been hiding in a different village, but the Mazureks seem like a safer family than the one with which she's been staying. Lola tells us that her husband, daughter, and son are all hiding elsewhere. Her son, however, is hiding outdoors on the roof of a barn because they do not have any money with which to pay anyone to hide him. Because of his exposure to the elements, he is getting sick, and she is very worried about him. To hide him in a warmer place, she asks if we can share some of our gold coins with her. We gladly give her a few of the coins, and thus she is able to arrange a better hiding place for her son.

When the spring arrives, it is easier to exercise during the evenings. One night we emerge from the pit and spot cattle cars in the distance. The next day the Mazureks tell us that these trains had been filled with Hungarian Jews, who were packed tightly in the cars and were calling out for water and food.[2] A chill runs down my spine. Could the Germans still be sending Jews to the gas chambers? Despite our revolt could they have rebuilt Sobibór? Doubt and regret plague me throughout the night. We have escaped from Sobibór, but could we be doing more to save others from the gas chambers? Should we find a new group of partisans with whom we can fight against the Germans? No, I know that based on our past experience in the woods, it is far too dangerous to leave the Mazureks. They are the only ones we can trust at this moment.

Late one afternoon we hear an explosion from the direction of the train tracks. We peek outside the barn and can see that a German cargo train has been derailed. This means that most likely a group of partisan saboteurs has succeeded in interrupting the Germans' supply line with the eastern front. We are overjoyed. But the following morning, Mrs. Mazurek enters the barn and frantically tells us, "The Germans have surrounded the village! The soldiers are going house to house, searching for the partisans! We are all going to the priest's house. Hopefully he will protect us. This is the only food I will be able to bring to you today. God help you all!"

We immediately take refuge in the pit and cover our heads with as much hay as possible. Only a few minutes later we hear the sound of boots walking above us in the barn. A German voice calls out, "Come out! Come out!"

I am seized by a choking fear. How have the Germans found us? What should we do now? We still have with us the guns that we stole from Sobibór, but our situation is hopeless. We can shoot the soldiers the moment that they uncover our hiding place, but reinforcements will undoubtedly arrive to throw a grenade into the pit. We decide to stay put as long as the hay remains on top of us. We aim our guns at the opening to the pit, try not to breathe, and pray for a miracle with all our might.

Then we hear a gunshot. But it has not been fired at us. A German soldier has shot a rabbit in the barn. It is the rabbit, not us, he had called out to!

Another few tense moments go by. Then just as abruptly as the Germans had arrived, they leave the barn. We are safe.

The next day Mr. Mazurek tells us that when the Germans had descended on the village, most of the other villagers had also fled to the priest's house in fear for their lives. Apparently the Germans had not found the partisans whom they sought. Mr. Mazurek is obviously relieved. But for the first time since we have known him, we can also see that he is scared. Had the Germans found us in the barn, it would have meant the death penalty for Mr. Mazurek and his family. From the moment we arrived, we have known that the Mazureks are risking their lives to save us. But now we understand that their heroism has never meant that they have overcome their fears; rather, they have been acting heroically while still in the presence of their fears. And now they are surely all the more aware of the threat that our continued presence poses to their lives. We worry that they might lose their courage and decide to kick us out.

Perhaps this is why soon after the raid, Aaron abruptly announces that he is going back to Oszczyce. He refuses to tell us why he is going. He only says that he will return that night and that he will take the route along the railroad tracks. Maybe he has some business to settle. Or maybe he wants to see if he can hide with his friend once more. He leaves around midnight, carrying the gun that he has stolen from Sobibór. The following night we hear a gun battle near the tracks about a quarter mile away. We fear the worst. The next day Mr. Mazurek tells us that Aaron's body has been found by people from the village. We can only guess whether it was Germans or bandits who have killed him.

Mr. Mazurek also informs us that, from now on, he refuses to accept any payment from us. He apparently wishes to save us from Aaron's fate. We now understand that our survival means far more to Mr. Mazurek than money. After so many others have either turned their backs on us or tried to kill us, we have drastically underestimated both him and his wife. These are two truly righteous people. Mr. and Mrs. Mazurek see us not as Jews but rather as human beings. They have nurtured their love of their brother at a time when many others are acting only out of fear, self-preservation, greed, or hate. We are grateful for Mr. and Mrs. Mazurek and inspired with hope.

Our lives in hiding continue without any interruptions for the next few months. Each day we feel one step closer to freedom and our strength grows. Then, in July 1944, we hear explosions in the distance. As the sounds rapidly grow in frequency, it is clear that a large battle is being fought. The eastern front is finally approaching! Our excitement grows as the battle draws closer and closer to us. Within just a few hours, we hear tanks and trucks driving along the main road of the village. Moments later Mrs. Mazurek enters the barn, holding a pail full of food for us as usual. But she is bringing more than just food today. "Come out!" she says. "The Soviets have taken control of the village!" We must see it to believe it. We climb out of the pit and behold the Soviet tanks advancing past us, toward Izbica. It is the happiest moment of my life. We all hug and cry tears of relief, joy, and sorrow.

12

Liberation and Victory

I emerge from our hiding place along with Symcha and Lola. Finally after almost five years of life under the Germans, I have regained the sensation of freedom. And I appreciate it as never before. My first steps feel both light and determined. Even the familiar sight of the village around me, with its scattered farms surrounded by the forest in the distance, seems suddenly beautiful.

We inform the Mazureks that we will be leaving and thank them one last time. They give us several blankets and sandwiches. We then walk to the main road and try to mix with the fighters and returning refugees. We do not know if Izbica, which is north of us, has yet been liberated from German control, so we decide to head south toward Zamość. Because the tanks are advancing from the road that originates in Zamość, we can be almost certain that by now it is under Soviet control. To get there we begin walking along the road. Despite the energy we have gained from knowing we are free, we soon grow rather weary. Eventually a farmer in a wagon drives by, and we ask for a ride to Zamość. The farmer agrees. Symcha and I load our belongings onto the wagon. But before we can climb onto the wagon ourselves, the farmer begins to drive away without us! We are far too weak to give chase. Ten minutes later a Soviet military truck approaches. Incredibly, the driver calls out to us in Yiddish!

"Do you need some help?" asks the friendly Soviet Jewish officer.

We tell him of how we have just been robbed and that we are looking for someone to drive us to Zamość.

"Get into the truck and come with me then," our newfound guardian angel says without hesitating.

He turns the truck around in the direction that the thief has headed. Within minutes our truck has caught up with the thief's wagon.

"Is he the one?" asks our driver.

We take a close look. It is indeed the same man. The officer stops the truck and springs outside to confront the culprit. As we look on from inside the vehicle, the officer strikes the thief and proceeds to recover all our belongings. And upon further inspection of the thief's wagon, the soldier finds an entire slaughtered cow hidden inside. It has been cut into quarters. He asks us for help removing the booty and placing it onto his truck. Even working together we barely have enough strength to lift each part of the cow. But somehow we manage to transfer the entire cow onto the truck.

Once we are all back on the truck, we think the officer will continue driving us to Zamość. Instead he begins to turn the truck around. Apparently he has different plans.

"What are you doing?" we ask.

"I must deliver these supplies to the front!" the officer answers.

We have no choice but to go along for what we know can be a dangerous ride. The officer turns around on the narrow stretch of road—we are certain that the truck will get caught in a ditch, but somehow he maneuvers successfully—and we begin our journey toward the battlefields.

"How active is the front?" we ask, not even sure that we want to know the answer.

"The Germans are retreating, but they are still fighting back."

The officer's answer does little to encourage us. After riding for about three miles, we can hear what sounds like rockets raining down in the distance. They each whir frighteningly as they travel through the air above our heads and plunge toward their targets. We are in the thick of a pitched battle. All I can think is: "I survived Sobibór, and now I am going to die on the eastern front!"

But our Soviet officer is undeterred. As we sweat it out in the truck, he hurriedly delivers the supplies and the cow. Then at last he turns the truck around. He drives us all the way to Zamość.

When we arrive, we thank the officer profusely. In Zamość we quickly find that about twenty-five Jews have grouped together in a community center called the Perec House.[1] Everyone is busy trading stories of how he or she has survived and of how many others have not. I am elated to find my friend Motel Altman at the house. He had used fake identification papers to live as a Catholic until he was liberated.

We stay at the Perec House for several weeks, enjoying hot meals from the communal kitchen, waiting for news, and discussing what to do next. Then one night someone throws an object that breaks the window of the room in which we are eating. After hearing the glass shatter, I immediately look and see something rolling on the floor about twenty feet from me. "Grenade!" we all cry out. We scurry out of the house as fast as we can. For some reason the grenade malfunctions, sparing all of us from being either killed or maimed. Despite our luck, it is clear that we are not yet truly out of the woods. Symcha and I decide that, from now on, I will stay at the large apartment of Symcha's new girlfriend, Lola, a native of Zamość to whom he has recently been introduced and with whom he is now living.

The next day I pick up Motel from the Perec House to shop for food together and to at least enjoy some of our newfound freedom. Just outside the Perec House, however, a Polish policeman stops us and asks for our identity documents. We explain that we don't have any papers because we are Jews who have lost everything during the war. Without asking any further questions, he promptly brings us to the Soviet authorities and proceeds to tell them that we are Germans! We can only guess that the policeman is intent on framing us because he hates Jews.

The Soviets promptly separate Symcha and me. They bring me to a dark interrogation room, where an interrogator politely says to me, "Tell me what you did during the war."

"I am a Jew from Izbica," I answer. "I escaped from Sobibór."

"Do not lie to me!" he yells before punching me in the nose. Blood flows. Surely my nose is broken. But I can't do anything other than protest my legitimate innocence.

"I am a Jew, I am a Jew," I repeat.

"You are not the first nationalist to tell me this," he says.

"You don't know what you are doing," I cry out. "The policeman who brought me here was probably a Nazi collaborator!"

My pleas are to no avail. The interrogator calls in the guards, who place me in a squalid, underground jail cell along with Symcha, who has also been beaten up. There are several others in the room, all of whom look like hardened criminals. In order to protect ourselves, Symcha and I take turns staying awake throughout the night. I think to myself that after the miracle of our survival and the way we had fought at Sobibór, I had expected to be paraded on a horse and carriage from town to town, but how naive I have been!

The next day the Soviets free us without any explanation. Outside the prison Lola is waiting. She says that she has pleaded with the authorities, successfully convincing them that Symcha and I are innocent Jews who had been framed by anti-Communist Polish nationalists.

Our thoughts turn to Izbica. By now the Soviets must have marched through and liberated it. We need to be wary of how our neighbors will treat us upon our return—some of them have likely taken over our homes and possessions—but we must at least try to return. It would be just as dangerous, we feel, to continue living in Zamość, where we have already had several close calls.

Symcha and I travel to Izbica. It is as we had left it, except that nearly all the houses are empty, and we do not see a single Jewish person on the streets. I shudder as I walk, knowing that on these same streets the blood of thousands of people has been spilled. Izbica feels to me more like a cemetery than a town.

Soon after our arrival, several townspeople begin following us around. But they do not say anything. They just go wherever we go, as if they are monitoring us. Then, with each passing minute, the crowd grows. We begin to feel uneasy. So instead of exploring the town further, we hastily agree to get right down to business: Symcha will go to the pharmacy to see if his services are needed, and I will go to visit the cemetery, where we believe that our mother had been shot. I want to see if anyone living near the cemetery can tell us anything more about what happened to her. Naturally, I would also like to see our old house and to recover the letter that Mr. Rosenberger asked me to hide in the ground. But we cannot go to our old house without first finding out if it is safe to do so. If someone else has assumed ownership of the house while we have been away, then attempting to reclaim our property can endanger us. Symcha plans to ask his friends in town for more information.

I begin walking toward the cemetery. As I near the hill leading to the gate, however, I spot one of my former classmates running toward me. In his right hand is a pistol. He is a boy I had not known very well during our youth. Now he seems almost crazed. Can he be trying to kill me? I start to run as fast as I can toward the police station, which is only about a quarter mile away and which I guess might now be the Soviet military headquarters. The boy gives chase, but I am able to outrun him.

When I reach the safety of the police station, Symcha is there, too. He has also been threatened by townspeople. We tell the Soviet officer in command at the station that we have survived the war but now feel unable to even walk through our own hometown. The officer proceeds to explain that he is helpless to assist us. "There is a Polish government with a Polish army now," he says, "and we cannot protect you here. Go to a big city. You will be safer there. Nobody will recognize you." The officer gives us a few grenades and instructs us on how to use them. Finally, he puts us on a Soviet military truck and tells the driver to drop us off in Lublin.

Because Warsaw is still under German control, Lublin has been named the new capital of Poland. With all the economic and political activity that this might bring to Lublin, it indeed seems the safest place for us to be. Furthermore, we have heard at the Perec House that my friend Mojsze Blank from Izbica has taken over the management of a leather factory in Lublin. The Soviets have appropriated it, and they need him to manage it. With what we know of the leather business, we think that he might hire us. So we go to his apartment, which we know is located at 4 Kowalska Street.

Mojsze greets us very warmly but tells us that unfortunately he does not have any work for us at the moment. He says we can stay with him for as long as we need. Symcha tells Mojsze that he prefers to return to Zamość the next day to look for work closer to his girlfriend's house. I tell Mojsze that I will stay a few days to see if there is any work for me elsewhere in Lublin. Late that evening there is a knock on Mojsze's door. Someone says in Yiddish, "Mojsze, open the door." He opens it. A group of men shouting at us in Polish rush in with pistols and begin beating and robbing us. I try to jump out of the first-floor window. But they grab me by the neck and pull me back into the room. They take everything they can find—which is not much—then run away. They don't shoot us because we are on a main street and they are probably worried that Soviet military forces can catch them. The next day I decide to head back to Zamość with Symcha. Not even the capital of Poland is safe at this moment.

Although we are now staying with Lola, we gather regularly at the Perec House to socialize with other survivors and to learn news of the war's progress. On one of our first visits to the Perec House after our return from Lublin, someone hands me and Symcha a letter that has been delivered from the city hall of Izbica. The letter is addressed to the mayor of Izbica, but it has been forwarded to the Perec House, for the reason that we discover when we read it:

> Dear Mayor,
> I am a citizen of Izbica who fled from the town soon after the war began. I left all my family behind. I am now living in the city of Lwów. I would simply like to know: Is anybody still alive?
> Sincerely,
> Jakub Białowicz

Our brother is alive! Someone in Izbica's city hall had sent the letter to Zamość, because he or she must have heard that Jewish survivors are assembling in the Perec House. We immediately send a letter to the address provided by Jakub. We tell him where we have been and advise him to join us as soon as possible. We choose not to tell him about all that has happened, that we three brothers are the only members of our family still alive. When Jakub writes back to us at the Perec House several weeks later, he tells us he will join us and informs us of exactly when he plans to arrive at the train station in Zamość. It will be in just a few days.

Symcha and I go together to the train station to see our brother for the first time in nearly five years. When he steps off the train, Jakub looks a little older but otherwise quite healthy. He is accompanied by his wife, a beautiful brunette.

We rush to greet them. Jakub can barely recognize me now that I have become a man. As we hug beside the train tracks, he says incredulously, "This is you, Fiszel? This is you?"

"It's me."

"And Mom and Dad? And Brancha, Rywka, and Toba? What happened to them?"

Symcha and I begin to cry. "They perished. Mom was shot in the cemetery. Everyone else perished in the camps." We all embrace and cry for several minutes. Jakub's wife tries to console him, but she is crying, too.

"Symcha, Fiszel, this is my wife, Ada."

"Welcome to our family," Symcha says.

We are not only welcoming Ada to our family, I tell myself, we are welcoming her to the only family that we still have. "It's nice to meet you both," says Ada. "Jakub has told me so much about the two of you."

Ada immediately strikes me as very mature and composed. She also seems a very good match for my independent-thinking brother. "So, Jakub, you did not even invite us to the wedding?" I joke.

We all share a much-needed laugh. "Come on, let's go eat," Symcha says.

Over a lunch of sandwiches, coffee, and cake, Jakub explains that after he crossed the Bug River, he had traveled all the way to Moscow, where he had found work at the Astronomical Institute. Then, before the Germans laid siege to the city, the Soviets had moved the entire institute to Dzhambul, Kazakhstan. There he had been able to live safely through the war. In Dzhambul he had also met Ada, who is a Polish Jew from Zamość. Jakub says he had recognized Ada because he used to ride his bicycle to Zamość to see movies and attend dances in the park. Being four years older than Jakub and already having a boyfriend, Ada says she had never noticed him. Like Jakub, however, she had escaped to the Soviet Union when the Germans came. They had married soon after they first met.

Jakub reports that most other Polish Jews had not been so lucky. After arriving in the Soviet Union, many had found life to be so difficult there that they had decided to apply to the Soviet authorities for permission to return to Nazi-occupied Poland. These unfortunate Jews were in turn accused of counterrevolutionary activity and sent by Stalin's paranoid government to prison camps! However, with our region no longer occupied by Nazis, it is safer to apply for repatriation, so Jakub had registered with the Soviet authorities and received permission to return.

Though we are lucky to be able to live in Lola's house for the time being, we still need to find some way to feed ourselves. My friend Motel and I decide to go into business together as traders. For this we will need to travel to Lublin to purchase items that we can then trade in other places. So we travel by bus to Lublin. Shortly before arriving in Lublin, however, our bus is stopped by what appears to be uniformed Polish policemen. We notice that several other buses in front of us have also been stopped. As I look out the window, I see dozens of people who appear to be Jewish being pulled from their buses. Then they are shot. For whatever reason no one approaches our bus, and after about ten tension-filled minutes of waiting, we are allowed to pass.

Despite the apparent danger, the need to support ourselves remains. We thus decide to go forward with our plan. Upon arriving in Lublin, we buy produce, meats, coffee, and cigarettes at the markets. We bring the goods back to Zamość and exchange them for clothing and money. We earn enough to support ourselves for a few weeks before making the same trip to Lublin to sell the clothes and again purchase goods that we bring back to Zamość.

We continue trading successfully for several months. Then, in January 1945, news arrives that the Soviets have finally liberated Warsaw. The allure—both cultural and economic—of Poland's new capital is too much for Motel and me to resist. I am also eager to search for several of my cousins who had lived in Warsaw before the war. We immediately head for the big city.

Upon arriving in Warsaw, we find nearly complete ruins. People confirm the news reports we had heard in Lublin about how the citizens of Warsaw had fought the Germans bravely for two entire months, while Soviet troops waited outside the city and offered no help. Some of Warsaw's few surviving Jews had fought alongside the remaining Poles, many of whom were members of the AK. After the Germans finally quelled the general uprising, they had proceeded to systematically firebomb the few buildings that had withstood the invasion of 1939, the Warsaw Ghetto uprising, and the most recent general uprising.

Very little remains of the Warsaw that my brothers and sisters had told me so much about. We find a restaurant, order food, and begin eating. Then we notice that police have surrounded the building. They storm through the front door and arrest everyone at our table. They suspect that we are smugglers. Before they arrest us, however, I manage to stuff all my money into a vase near our table. For a few days they interrogate us. I tell them I am just a survivor who is trying to find a place to live. They cannot find anything in our clothes, so they free us. The first thing I do is run back to the restaurant, where upon my return I find that my money is still in the vase!

We return to Lublin, where Mojsze has incredible news to share: the authorities have caught one of the Germans who had supervised the mass murders at the Majdanek concentration camp. He will be publicly executed tomorrow. The plan is to march him from Lublin to Majdanek, which is just outside the center of the city. There he will be hanged for all to see. The next day Mojsze and I walk in a procession with thousands of other people who have also come out to witness the punishment. After placing the noose around the German's neck, the executioner initiates the hanging. But the noose somehow fails to work. So the executioner attempts to reposition it. After he fumbles with the noose for a few moments, the condemned man grabs the rope, tightens it himself, and shouts in German: "Damned Poles, you can't even hang a person!" This time it works. Mojsze and I rejoice along with the rest of the crowd.

Our happiness, however, is soon mixed with sorrow. We receive news from Szlome Lerer—who has also survived Sobibór—that the coleader of the revolt, Leon Feldhendler, has been murdered. Leon had been running a leather factory in Lublin, where he employed many young survivors of the war, including Szlome. He has been shot by unknown assailants. Nobody knows the motive for the murder. However, judging from the examples of hatred that we have seen expressed toward Jews, we guess that Leon has been murdered because he was a prominent Jew who was helping other Jews to live.[2]

On May 8, 1945, I join several other survivors of Sobibór, including one of Aaron Licht's relatives, for dinner in Lublin. Our spirits are full of hope because, during each of the past several days, we have listened to incredible reports about German troops surrendering one after another, even in Italy and Berlin. We talk of how good it feels to know that the war is coming to an end. Late in the evening, we are still eating and talking when someone enters the room and says, "Did you hear the news? The Germans have surrendered completely!"

At last the war is truly over. It is a bittersweet moment. We have all lost so many relatives and friends. Our homes are gone. We know that these emotional wounds will never heal fully, but at this moment our gratitude for life overwhelms us. We hail our victory over the Nazis by drinking countless shots of vodka, each one loudly accompanied by the traditional Jewish toast, "L'chaim!"[3]

13 |

Life as a Displaced Person

Now that I am finally free, where am I to go? Back to Izbica? A sweet thought when I remember life before the war, but there is no going back, nothing to go back to. The living nightmare I had experienced in Izbica has left a traumatic impression on me. I know the town of my birth will always be a place of mourning to me. The Nazi war machine has been stopped, but not before it had changed Izbica—and the rest of Poland—into something I can barely recognize anymore. Nearly every Jew from Izbica has perished. Who knows how many Jews in all of Poland have survived the war?[1] Of the survivors whom I know, many are alone in the world. Despite all the suffering I have endured, I tell myself, I am relatively fortunate to still have my two brothers.

We understand that it will take a long time for life to return to a sense of normalcy. But we can begin taking small steps toward rebuilding our lives and maybe even leaving Poland to pursue our dream of a better future in Palestine. Jakub and Ada decide to go to Łódź because Ada had worked there for her uncle before the war and has many acquaintances whom she can rely on for help. Symcha and Lola marry each other in a small ceremony. They hear that in the city of Wałbrzych it will be possible to move into one of the apartments of the ethnic Germans, who have either fled or been deported to Germany. The Polish municipalities are assigning the apartments. Supposedly almost anyone can receive one. So Symcha and Lola decide to try their luck. I go along with them for the trip and pack some goods from Lublin that I plan to sell or trade in Wałbrzych.

All goes well in Wałbrzych until my return trip to Lublin. Upon buying my train ticket at the station in Wałbrzych, I find that the train is full.

However, the conductor tells me to come with him, promising that he'll find me a place. He puts me in an equipment room beneath the train. Though it's uncomfortable, I know that I can manage until the end of the trip. Then the conductor locks the door from the outside. This alarms me, but once again I tell myself that I will manage. When we arrive in Lublin, however, the conductor doesn't return to unlock the door. I figure that either he wants to leave me to die there, or he will come later to rob me of my belongings when no one is near the train. I start yelling and banging. Fortunately some workers come and release me. I head straight for Mojsze's house, wondering if my life has just been saved again.

By summertime we hear that the Allies have created displaced persons (DP) camps where relief is being provided to war victims who have lost their homes. The closest such camps are in occupied Germany. Conditions inside the camps are reportedly not perfect—some of them are even located on the sites of the Nazis' former concentration camps at Dachau and Bergen-Belsen—but apparently they are at least free of the violence that we are witnessing in Poland. Smugglers from whom I buy food tell me that the Polish–German border is guarded only lightly. It seems as if the Soviets want Jews in Poland to flee to the care of the Americans and the British in occupied Germany. After discussing it with Symcha and Jakub, I resolve to sneak across Poland's western border to live in one of the DP camps in occupied Germany. My destination will be Berlin, where, I have heard, a large camp has been created at Schlactensee. After confirming that conditions are livable, I will return to bring Symcha, Jakub, and their wives back with me.

But before I leave Poland perhaps forever, Symcha and I decide to attempt to recover the jewels that we had left behind in Sobibór. We also plan to visit Siedliszcze, the hometown of our father's two brothers and their families prior to the war, to see if anyone else from our family remains. First we reach the woods just a few miles from Sobibór. But in the distance we hear the sounds of a battle raging. Perhaps there are anti-Communist partisan groups still fighting against the Soviets in this region. Even if we can somehow avoid the fighting, the mines surrounding Sobibór are probably still active. I tell Symcha, "We survived Sobibór. Let's not be killed just for the sake of these jewels." Symcha agrees. We give up our search, back away in honor of life, and head for Siedliszcze.

Siedliszcze had been a predominantly Jewish town of about fifteen hundred people before the war. But when we arrive, we do not see a single Jew on the streets. We walk past our uncles' homes, but there is no sign of them anywhere. Their homes are now occupied by other families.

Leaving Symcha behind, I travel by train to the border at Szczecin. There I give money and vodka to a Soviet soldier, who agrees to transport me by truck into occupied Germany. After he drops me off on the other side of the border, I walk through some small towns, and then hop on a train to Berlin, where I am directed to the Schlactensee Camp for Displaced Persons. Upon entering the camp, I think to myself that Herta had been right: I have ended up in Germany after the war. But no matter what I am to find in Germany, I know that I do not want to stay permanently. I still want to go to Palestine, where I can make a new life for myself in freedom, without seeing Germans every day. Simply hearing the German language is too much to bear. It reminds me of the murderers and the many beloved people I have lost, especially Herta.

At the DP camp, I find myself sleeping in military-style barracks for the first time since I had been at Sobibór, but it does not bother me. I am free, I am safe, and I am beginning a new life, alongside hundreds of other survivors who have lost just as much as I have. A few days after arriving at Schlactensee, however, I hear about another camp called Neu Freimann, near Munich. Supposedly it has better services and accommodations than the camp at Schlactensee. I decide to at least visit this place to compare it to Schlactensee. After a train trip of several hours, I arrive in Munich. There I make my way to a community center, where I hear that Jewish refugees can receive food and financial support. While standing on the steps, I recognize a passerby: he is an SS officer from Sobibór! His name is Nowak. I yell to the people beside me, "That man is an SS officer from Sobibór! Let's get him!" Nowak immediately flees. Along with a few other refugees, I give chase. We find a German police officer, who also runs after Nowak. But the criminal blends into the crowd of people. He is gone, and there is little more that we can do.

I spend several weeks at Neu Freimann, which is indeed nicer than Schlactensee because it has small houses rather than barracks. I also find a few of my old friends there. Together we enjoy the camp and the pockets of liveliness that remain in Munich despite the city's widespread destruction caused by the war's air raids. But I cannot stay for long. It is time to bring Symcha, Jakub, and their wives to the safety of Germany. But to do so I will need to return to Poland because I want to help them make the trip. So I register myself for a repatriation program for Polish people returning from Germany to Poland.

I return to Poland and successfully bring Symcha, Lola, Jakub, and Ada back to Germany. We end up being placed at Schlactensee, where we and many of our fellow survivors immediately devote ourselves to life. We dance, make music, tell jokes, stage productions, and form political groups. Many people start new families. David Ben-Gurion himself comes to visit the camp one day, and, along with nearly everyone else, I crowd into a lecture hall to listen to a speech that he delivers about how we can all help to develop Palestine through life on a kibbutz. It is a nice dream to have, I tell myself, but I still believe that the British will not allow a Jewish state in Palestine unless we fight for it and win it from them.

Near the end of 1947, after almost a year spent in Schlactensee, the camp begins to close down and we are transferred to a DP camp in Heidenheim. There Jakub and Symcha quickly assume leadership positions. Jakub joins the presidium of the DP camp, and Symcha becomes a sports director. Jakub convinces me to attend dentistry classes offered in the mornings by the Organization for Rehabilitation through Training (ORT), and to do an apprenticeship in the afternoons under a dentist named Martin Priss. A German dental technician tells me that Dr. Priss is a former Nazi district supervisor who had been arrested during the "de-Nazification" process. However, according to the technician, after Dr. Priss's release he had vowed to rehabilitate himself through kindness to Jews. Dr. Priss trains me well and allows me to rapidly assume important responsibilities, such as performing fillings and root canals. He even invites me to many enjoyable dinners at his house. Despite his past I come to know and respect both Dr. Priss and his entire family.

I begin to enjoy the stability that still eludes some of my friends. At a dance held at the DP camp, I am smitten by a lovely woman named Mala who becomes my girlfriend. She is a Polish Jew who has worked as a secretary in the DP camp's presidium office. Mala and her family had survived the war by fleeing to the Soviet Union. She is extremely bright, as well as blonde haired and very beautiful.

Despite the happiness that I am starting to enjoy in the DP camp, like nearly everyone else I do not plan to live out the rest of my life in Germany. My dream remains focused on starting a new life in Palestine, if only the British will lift the restrictions that prevent us from immigrating to its shores. Others are not so patient: at the urging of Irgun representatives who visit the DP camps to raise money and enlist recruits, several of my friends decide to embark upon the clandestine journey to Palestine by land and sea.[2] They plan to pressure the British administration in Palestine by helping the Irgun to attack British military and government targets. I support my friends by performing much-needed dental work for them before their journey. I wish that I can join them, but the Irgun representatives encourage me to support their cause by continuing to treat my friends. I also donate money to the Irgun whenever I can. And I participate in peaceful demonstrations urging that the DP camps be speedily closed and that we be repatriated to Palestine.

In November of 1947 we are all encouraged by the announcement of the United Nations' Partition Plan for Palestine that calls for British withdrawal from the territory and the official establishment of a Jewish state alongside an Arab state. But the leaders of the Arab community reject the plan and begin attacks on Jewish targets. The fighting escalates in May of 1948 when British forces announce their intention to withdraw, Jewish leaders declare a new independent state called Israel, and several Arab armies invade the new state. Each day I listen to the radio reports with intense concern. Everyone in the camp actively monitors and discusses the war until the fighting at last ends in the middle of 1949, with Israel as the victor. The ability of Israel's small army to fight off the much larger armies that tried to destroy it appears to me like the miracle that saved my own life at Sobibór. It is an incredible relief for everyone in the camp. It also means that I can finally immigrate to Israel.

After two years of apprenticing under Dr. Priss, I still require more training but I feel that I have enough experience to perform some dental procedures for people in addition to my friends. I also want to earn enough money to establish myself once I go to Israel. So I ask Jakub to assign me a slightly larger apartment, where I then set up an office and perform basic dental work on many patients before their emigration to Israel. For more complicated cases such as wisdom-teeth extractions, I arrange with a German dentist to treat the patients every Wednesday for two hours. I pay him 200 marks each week. I start to make some money and am able to buy two motorcycles, one a BMW and the other a DKV. Mala and I ride motorcycles through the countryside around Heidenheim about twice a week. We also go on skiing vacations in Garmisch, which had been the site of the 1936 Winter Olympics. We are in love and want to marry, but only if we can move to Argentina, where her uncle now lives and has a business in Buenos Aires. But my heart is set on Israel. So she moves to Argentina without me. I am disappointed, but I start dating her friend Lucia Metzmacher, who is very interested in me. She has survived several concentration camps, and discussing our similar experiences helps us to grow very close. She gives me thoughtful presents including a silver cigarette holder with my initials.

By now several of my friends have successfully emigrated from the DP camp to Israel with barely half the dental experience that I have, and yet they have managed to open thriving offices of their own. They write from Israel, encouraging me to join them. Soon my brothers also immigrate to Israel. I am prepared to join them but have commitments to finish dental work on several patients, so I decide to join my brothers later. Shortly after they arrive in Israel, however, they send me a letter begging me not to follow them because another war with the Arab nations is still a real possibility. They urge me to go to the United States, where the government has recently relaxed some of its strict immigration quotas, where I can be safe, and where we will know that at least one member of the Białowicz family will survive to carry on the family name.

I know that my brothers are right. In spite of the U.S. government's blindness and cruelty in turning back some of the ships carrying desperate Jewish refugees during the war, I understand that the United States is still a great country of freedom and opportunity. I hope that it will ultimately provide a safe and peaceful environment for me. So I apply for resettlement in the United States. While I am waiting for my application to be processed, the Heidenheim DP camp closes. Lucia decides to go to Canada, where she already has family to receive her. I transfer to the Landsberg DP camp, where I establish another dental office and live for several months until I receive word that the United States has accepted my residency application.

In the spring of 1950 I leave Europe behind and embark upon a new life in the United States. I sail across the Atlantic to Boston, Massachusetts. After the immigration proceedings at the port, I am greeted by a representative of the Joint Distribution Committee (JDC). On the same day, she puts me on a train to Columbus, Ohio, where she says the JDC plans to resettle me. She presents me with a package of food, including chewing gum, for my trip.

Another representative of the JDC greets me at the train station in Columbus. She brings me to her office, where she tells me that from my records, she knows that I have experience in the dental profession. "However," she informs me, "we have many dentists in America, and it will be easier to find work as a dental technician." She says she will look for a job for me. She assigns me a room with a family in a private home owned by an elderly American Jewish widow, Mrs. Silverback, who provides meals and speaks to me in Yiddish.

I am given seventeen dollars per week to cover my room and board until I can find a paying job. Within a few weeks, the woman from the JDC finds a position for me at a dental lab. As soon as I receive my first paycheck, the agency stops providing me with the weekly allowance. Now I am really on my own.

14

Resettling in the United States

I yearn to be a dentist, not a technician. So I ask the owner of the dental lab for advice on bettering my position. That's when I discover that my German credentials are not valid in America. To do the same level of work here, I will need to pay for classes and certifications with money I do not have. This is a major setback for my dream of successful resettlement. I have no choice but to seek additional work in the hopes of earning and saving enough money to eventually attend a dental school. So I start an additional, part-time job doing inventory control at the giant Lazarus Department Store. I also see that a local shoe store, Schiff's, is hiring part-time workers, and I convince the manager to give me a chance in spite of my limited ability to speak English.

I do well at the job of selling shoes and am soon considered for a managerial position. Within a few months, I have also secured bank credit by saying, "My aim is to be in the dental line," and have saved enough money to afford the first payments on a new car, a beautiful white Chevrolet that I am proud to drive. I drive the car to the boarding house and park in front.

When I enter the house, Mrs. Silverback is surprised to see my new car parked outside. "My son has lived here all his life," she says, "and he could never afford to have such a car. You come here and after a few months you have this car? How did you manage to do this?"

Even with a car, however, I have very little social life in Columbus. The city has only a tiny Jewish community. I am twenty-four, and I want to be among friends. Ever since my arrival in Columbus, Lucia has sent me numerous letters inviting me to Toronto, in Canada, where she has resettled. I strongly consider going there to renew our relationship. But I wait too long and she marries someone else. It breaks my heart, but I am still happy for Lucia. I decide to visit her and her new husband while at the same time exploring cities in which I can live with larger Jewish populations. So I inform my bosses that I am taking a vacation and head off on a road trip to Toronto and New York City. In both places I can visit many people whom I first met in the DP camps.

I have a wonderful time reminiscing with my old friends. But these are just memories, and I need the opportunity to make new ones. In New York I take note of the many other survivors thriving in the big city. I know that I must move there.

When I return to Columbus and tell the owner of the dental lab that I am leaving, he tells me that he would like me to stay. "Philip," he says, "you're like a member of the family. We like you very much and sooner or later you'll be taking over. I can see you running the business someday." I thank him for all he has done for me but explain that he cannot persuade me to stay because my decision is not about making a living. I just can't adjust to living in Ohio without having some friends and a social life. That's why I need to go.

The lab owner generously insists on providing me with money for two weeks of training, and he even pays for my train ticket. He also says that he'll always welcome me should I decide to return. "Anytime you decide to come back," he says, "the door is always open for you."

And so I leave Columbus behind, grateful for a start at earning my way but glad to move into something fresh and new in one of the world's greatest cities. New York is exciting with bustle, job opportunities, and a large Jewish population. Thanks to a good lead from one of my friends, I find a room in the apartment of a family on Kosciuszko Street in Brooklyn.

I quickly begin work as a dental technician at the respected Sternberg Dental Lab on Forty-sixth Street in Manhattan. After a few months, however, my desire to attend dental school begins to wane. I yearn to make a good living right away without waiting to complete years of training on a subject that, for the most part, I have already mastered. So I decide to scour the newspaper classifieds section for a better-paying job. When I see an ad placed by a jewelry manufacturing firm, the Suna Jewelry Company, I sense a golden opportunity. They need a jeweler. I have never done such work before, but I figure that I can get by with the soldering experience that I gained in the dental labs. So I take a chance and apply for the job. I tell the owner, who is somewhere in his sixties, that I have five years of experience when I actually don't even have five days.

"Come back Monday," he says, "and we'll try you out."

All weekend I don't sleep, worrying about Monday. But I know how to solder and hope that this will somehow get me through.

On the first day, the owner hands me a box filled with raw materials for creating models of jewelry—rings, bracelets, and earrings—from scratch. I don't know where to begin. I struggle through the day. I want to show that I can perform at least some of the tasks he has assigned me. Somehow I manage to use this tool and that to make the jewelry, though I know my lack of craftsmanship will be obvious when I display my work to the boss.

At 5:00 p.m. the workday ends, and I show the boss what I have accomplished. I am practically shaking with anxiety. He takes a look at my work and says, "It seems to me you only have three years of experience. This is good enough for me. Tomorrow you come to work."

I am immensely relieved, and over the following weeks, with a little bit of training, I learn the trade. After three or four months, the company makes me a manager. I work there for two years, until I have enough experience to go into business for myself.

Life in New York is all that I have hoped for. I enjoy great friendships, attend cultural and social events, and am generally much happier than I was in Columbus. The one great shock I experience during my first years in New York occurs when I come across a long story in the *New York Times* about a tragic accident involving a car that had been hit by a train at a crossing in Toronto. Killed in the accident was my ex-girlfriend Lucia, along with her husband. A baby girl whom they had left at home was now an orphan under the care of Lucia's sister.

From Brooklyn I journey to the new State of Israel to visit my brothers and their families. The year is 1953. Israel is a more stunning country than I had ever imagined. Everything casts a spell on me: the warm Tel Aviv air that smells of the blue Mediterranean, the green hills of Haifa, the vast Negev desert, and the symphony of Hebrew and Yiddish spoken in streets, cafés, and apartments. Though it is my first time in this country, I feel embraced by the soil of my ancestors. And I am not the only one. Despite ongoing threats of violence from neighboring Arab states, everywhere I look I see people beaming with determination and pioneering spirit. In these new Israelis I see the sunburned faces of the *chaluzim* who once chopped wood and studied Hebrew in Izbica, preparing for this day. I also see the hopeful faces of my friends from the displaced persons camps who once dreamed of this land and are finally here living out their dreams.

My brothers also feel comfortable and joyful in their new surroundings. They now have the full protection of Israel's armed forces. Moreover, if Jews are ever persecuted again anywhere in the world, it is comforting for me to know that now there is a country that will always offer a haven in which to find refuge. I am proud that my brothers are contributing so directly to the success of this incredible, young state. I am also grateful that I have lived to see this day. If only we could share this joy, I think to myself, with our lost family and friends.

When I visit Israel again in 1958, Symcha says I should find someone nice there to marry. He introduces me to a very pretty girl named Rela, who is seventeen years old. She had been born in the Soviet Union during the war, but her family was from Krakow. While we are dating, I wonder if she might be too young to marry. Trying to hurry me along, her mother tells me, "My daughter is in love with you." I love Rela too. We marry in Israel, and after waiting for approval from the United States, she joins me in the Bronx. At last, with my new wife in my new home country, I am finally able to find the peace that I have not enjoyed since I was a child.

Epilogue: Life after Sobibór

I was nineteen years old when the war ended in 1945, and I already knew I was a transformed person going forward in this world, thanks to all that I had experienced at the hands of the Nazi murderers. My childhood innocence had long ago vanished with the murders of nearly all my beloved family members and friends. As an impressionable teenager, I had learned that people are capable of unimaginable cruelty. Yet I had also witnessed inspirational acts of stunning heroism by both my fellow Jewish prisoners at Sobibór and the Catholic farmers who saved my life. No longer a hunted Jew, I gained the blessed freedom to live a life of meaning and joy—in short, a life that would honor the memories of my loved ones and the deeds of the heroes who saved me.

Liberty also meant trying to start fresh, creating some kind of normal life that by itself would represent a defeat of the Nazis, who had wanted to obliterate me and so many others. In spite of wartime barbarity and the millions who were murdered, those of us who had survived prevailed. We could settle in a safe place where our lives would not be threatened. We could find work, and even have children as a testimony to our survival. After losing nearly everything, including most of my family, the United States gave me an incredible opportunity—first in the displaced persons camps and subsequently as a U.S. citizen—to build a new family and to devote myself to bettering the world in whatever ways I could.

My New Family

During my nine years with Rela, we had two children: Simone (born 1961) and Jeffrey (born 1964). My second marriage, in 1970, was to Susan, who was a teacher and a third-generation American. We met each other at a Saturday night Purim wine-tasting at a synagogue in Manhattan. Together we had three children before we divorced: Evelyn (born 1971), Joseph (born 1974), and Michael (born 1978).

Everything changed for me and my family in 1986 when my daughter Evelyn was diagnosed with osteosarcoma, a particularly virulent type of bone cancer. After a long and painful battle with the illness, including many difficult treatments, she died in 1989. Evelyn was one of a kind. In the hospital, going through the experience of bone cancer, she was more concerned about me than herself. Knowing how fragile my own health was, she asked the doctor not to tell me about her illness. She shared poems with me on the phone. Once at 6:00 a.m., from inside her breathing apparatus and knowing that her cancer was spreading, she called to wish me a happy birthday and to say that she loved me.

During her illness, Evelyn wrote a beautiful piece that I am including here because it shows how loss, resilience, and hope were themes in her short life as well as mine. We both respected these qualities for the good they can do in the world.

"An Accomplishment of Mine"

By Evelyn Bialowitz

On October 3, 1986, I received the most devastating news I had ever heard. It was my fifteenth birthday and the date I was diagnosed with bone cancer. My life and the life of my friends and family would never be quite the same. Over the past two years I have gone through chemotherapy, several surgeries, and painful procedures, so I am no longer a stranger to physical pain. When I look back at the past two years, I realize that I have adopted an optimistic outlook toward life. Speaking from experience, this is not a simple task, and I feel it is an accomplishment that I can and should be proud of. When I was first diagnosed, one of the first questions I asked myself was, "Why me?" Although I still don't have the answer, people seem to have many ideas of their own. A good friend once told me that she thinks the reason is because I was so strong. When people tell me this, I tell them that when you are in my position, you have to be strong in order to cope. Another good friend of mine told me that the quality she admires in me most is my positive outlook. When things are not going my way, again I tell myself, I wish I didn't have to adopt a positive outlook, but when you have cancer you must. In my own opinion, I think I was chosen to go through all this in order to teach me something and possibly set a good example for others in my situation. Unfortunately, it is a hard lesson to learn. I am very proud of this accomplishment because it took so much to achieve. I believe the grass is always greener on the other side, and I am still fighting to get there.

Evelyn's essay appeared in a newsletter published by the Tomorrow's Children Fund, a support group for children with cancer and their families. The organization began at the Hackensack University Medical Center, where Evelyn received most of her care. I know that in the end, her writing and her life inspired not only me but also a great number of people inside and outside our family.

Being a father was and still is an extraordinary experience, especially after having once doubted if I would survive the war and be able to ever have a family. I have always tried to ensure that my children receive the opportunity to study—a luxury of which I was largely deprived by the war. I believe that each of my children, similar to numerous other children of Holocaust survivors, has been uniquely and profoundly influenced by my experience of the Holocaust. My daughter Simone immigrated to Israel, the place I once dreamed of living in when I was young, and returned to the strictly observant Jewish lifestyle that I grew up with. She has blessed me with twelve wonderful grandchildren. My youngest son, Michael, is a mensch who has blessed me with three grandchildren, including one whom he named Alexander in tribute to the coleader of the Sobibór revolt, Aleksandr "Sasha" Pechersky. My oldest son, Jeff, has devoted his life to teaching physical education to at-risk youths in New York City's public schools. My middle son, Joseph, has chosen to practice environmental management because it helps people to enjoy healthier lives, and he often lectures alongside me about the importance of Holocaust remembrance and education.

"When you teach your son," says the Talmud, "you teach your son's son." All my children know my history, and when I am gone, they will continue to tell the story. In a world where people still deny that the Holocaust even occurred, my children—more than anyone to whom I have told my story—are essential eyewitnesses to an eyewitness of the Holocaust.

I am tremendously proud of each of my children and grandchildren. My life and theirs together represent an everlasting victory over the Nazis. They validate all my many efforts to stay alive under the worst circumstances. This family life I owe, most of all, to Sasha Pechersky, Leon Feldhendler, the Mazurek family, and my brother Symcha.

Justice for the Nazi Perpetrators

Since the end of the war, I have closely followed the destinies of the Nazis who persecuted me. I learned that Izbica's German-appointed mayor, Jan Schultz, who was extremely cruel to both Jews and Poles during the war, was the first to be brought to justice. Because of his collaboration with the Germans, he was sentenced to death by the Polish underground resistance movement. They executed him in 1943, before the war even ended.[1] Kurt Engels, the bloodthirsty Gestapo officer from Izbica, ended up in Hamburg. There he cleverly opened a café in partnership with a Jew who did not know of Engels's war background. Soon afterward, he was recognized and arrested. He committed suicide in jail.

The murderers who escaped vengeance at Sobibór experienced highly diverse fates. After Sobibór was officially closed, many of its surviving SS officers were sent to Istria. There they helped to prepare the local Jewish population to be rounded up and taken to San Saba near Trieste, where the building of a crematorium was already in progress. However, the war ended before their plans could be carried out.[2]

After the war, the surviving Ukrainian guards (probably several hundred who served at Sobibór at various times) went into hiding, and most were never found. Many of them probably posed as innocent displaced persons and were able to immigrate legally, despite their war crimes, to democracies such as the United States, Canada, and Australia. Eighteen of them were eventually arrested and tried in the Soviet Union. Seventeen of these eighteen guards were executed, and one was sentenced to fifteen years in prison. Sasha Pechersky, who lived out the rest of his life in the

Soviet Union until his death in 1990, provided key testimony against these guards.[3]

As I write this in January 2010, I have just delivered testimony in Munich, Germany, at the trial of John Demjanjuk. He is accused of having served at Sobibór as one of the Ukrainian guards during roughly the same six-month period that I spent as a prisoner at the camp. I cannot recognize Mr. Demjanjuk, but neither can I remember the faces of most Sobibór guards. During the court proceedings I simply informed the German judges of the crimes that I had witnessed at Sobibór, including details of how the Ukrainian guards supervised, beat, and sometimes shot Jewish prisoners. Mr. Demjanjuk's attorney defended his client by saying that if he indeed served at Sobibór, it was only because he was a prisoner of war who would have been killed by the Germans if he did not follow their orders. Although this might have been true, no person faced with such a predicament gains the right to save oneself by beating or shooting innocent men, women, and children; even under duress there is always a moral responsibility to resist an immoral order. If the court determines that Mr. Demjanjuk served at Sobibór, then justice demands that he be punished appropriately either for what he did or—if specific acts cannot be proven—for serving at Sobibór for so many months without apparently resisting the orders that he received. Justice in this case will also send an important message to anyone who contemplates or helps to carry out genocide: you will be held accountable for your actions.

Several of the Nazis who served at Sobibór either committed suicide or escaped and were never brought to justice. One of the first Nazis to be apprehended was Hubert Gomerski, one of Sobibór's worst killers. Near the end of 1949 I was asked to travel to Frankfurt to testify against him at a pretrial hearing. When I entered the room, there was Gomerski, seated calmly and looking exactly the same as when I had last set eyes on him, six years earlier at Sobibór. I had been looking forward to the opportunity to help convict Gomerski, but nothing could prepare me for how I would react to seeing him again. The moment I saw him, a feeling of immense rage boiled up and quickly overtook me. My whole body started shaking. I began yelling, "You murderer! You killed my whole family! You killed thousands of people!" I picked up a chair and was about to throw it at him, but I was restrained by the guards. They told me that if I did not control myself I would end up like him. I called out to the judge, "Life in prison is not enough! He should be shot, he should be shot!"

In 1950 Gomerski, as well as an SS man who had operated the gas chambers, Erich Bauer, were both sentenced to life imprisonment. However, in 1971 Gomerski filed an appeal. I gave preliminary testimony in New York about him. I was then asked to travel to Germany for Gomerski's trial, but before I could depart I received a letter informing me that he had fallen ill and therefore the retrial had been canceled. I later discovered that because the retrial could not occur, Gomerski was for some reason freed from prison as well. Despite his purportedly grave illness, he lived until 1999, dying in complete freedom at the age of eighty-eight. Bauer died in Berlin-Tegel prison in 1980. At the same time that Gomerski and Bauer were sentenced in 1950, SS Unterscharführer Johann Klier, who was regarded as relatively humane by Sobibór's prisoners, was found not guilty.[4]

The second set of trials against Sobibór's SS staff began in 1965 in Hagen, West Germany, a small city near Köln (Cologne). On trial were Karl Frenzel as well as several lower-ranking SS men who had served with him. The sadistic Frenzel received the life sentence that he deserved. The lower-ranking men received sentences ranging from not guilty to eight years in prison. Among the men found guilty were Franz Wolf, Alfred Ittner, Werner Dubois, and Erich Fuchs.

The punishments given to Wolf, Ittner, Dubois, and Fuchs could have been more severe. And the freedom that Gomerski enjoyed in his later years will always upset me. Being allowed to serve anything less than life in prison after murdering hundreds of thousands of innocent men, women, and children was more than an injustice—it was a betrayal of the victims and a dangerous signal to future murderers that they can get off lightly for the most serious crimes imaginable.

Sobibór's most sadistic Nazi, Gustav Wagner, escaped after the war to Syria and then, in 1951, to Brazil. There he lived under his own name as a farmhand in the town of Attibaia until 1978, when the Brazilian media was tipped off to Wagner's presence by the renowned Nazi hunter Simon Wiesenthal. Fearing that he would be abducted and taken to Israel to stand trial like Adolf Eichmann, the sixty-six-year-old Wagner sought the protection of Brazilian authorities in São Paulo. Israel was the first country to file extradition papers, followed by Wagner's native Austria, then West Germany and Poland. Meanwhile, Wagner's photo appeared in the Brazilian newspapers and was seen by a former Sobibór prisoner, Stanislaw "Szlome" Szmajzner, who had settled in Brazil. Szmajzner immediately flew to São Paulo to positively identify Wagner and ensure that the criminal would remain in custody. In front of a gathering of reporters, Szmajzner confronted Wagner for the first time. "How are you, Gustl?" was how Szmajzner greeted Wagner, using the former officer's nickname from Sobibór. Wagner at first appeared unwilling or unable to recognize Szmajzner but, after some consideration, replied: "Yes, yes, I remember you well. I took you out of the transport and saved the lives of you and your two friends who were also goldsmiths." Szmajzner responded, "So, and my sister, my mother, my father, and my brothers? If you say that you saved my life, then you must have also known that others would die." Wagner did not reply. Surely he regretted his incriminating statement.[5]

Although Wagner admitted to having served at Sobibór, he maintained that he only supervised the construction of barracks at Sobibór and that no Jews were ever killed at the camp. But Wagner's public encounter with Sjmajzner in front of the press was enough to force the Brazilian authorities to detain Wagner. A legal battle over extradition ensued. Austria's extradition request was denied because Wagner had renounced his Austrian citizenship and the alleged crimes had not occurred in that country; the Polish request was turned down because its current judicial system was unacceptable under Brazilian law; and the Israeli request was rejected because Israel had not existed at the time when Wagner participated in the mass executions.

According to Brazilian law, only West Germany's extradition request was valid. But Brazil's Supreme Court blocked Wagner's extradition to West Germany because of a typographical error. The Brazilian Portuguese translation of West Germany's extradition papers incorrectly stated that Wagner had been on West Germany's wanted list since "1974" instead of "1947." Brazil's statute of limitations required that charges be issued no more than twenty years after commission of a crime.[6] Wagner was therefore freed on June 20, 1979.[7]

West Germany subsequently presented the Brazilian court with a properly typed translation of the extradition papers. But Wagner had already vanished.[8] He died in his home on October 3, 1980.[9] Official Brazilian records listed his cause of death as suicide. A photo of the dead Wagner, however, showed him on the floor of his bathroom, apparently bleeding from stab wounds to many parts of his body.[10] It looked more like the scene of a crime than a suicide. A possible cause of death was neither crime nor suicide, but justice: one of Sobibór's bravest fighters, Szmajzner, let on that he had not been an entirely passive bystander at Wagner's death.[11]

In 1983 I was asked to testify at the second war-crimes trial of Frenzel. After having been arrested in Germany in 1962 and sentenced in 1966 to life in prison, he had served only ten years before being released on a technicality. Now he was being retried.[12] Remembering him very well—too well—I felt a duty to be part of the prosecution. I left my family in the United States and headed back to Europe.

I did not know what to expect when I arrived in Germany. What I found were many extremely friendly people who went out of their way to comfort me during my stay in Hagen. A welcome committee greeted me at the airport. Other committee members came to my hotel to introduce themselves. In my hotel room, I found a note on the desk: "My name is Mrs. Keilwagen. I am a teacher in a local school and my husband is an architect. We are on the welcome committee. We know you will be going through difficult times for the trial, and we would like to make your stay as pleasant as we possibly can. At 7:00 p.m. tonight we are coming to pick you up and take you to dinner to welcome you officially." I was deeply moved by this welcome.

The Keilwagens took me to their house, where I saw a table decorated for an elaborate dinner in my honor. On the walls I saw many Jewish artifacts. I asked Mrs. Keilwagen, "What is this?"

"I teach religion," she said, "and I collect artifacts. Let me get my parents so they can meet you." I admit that I thought to myself: what if I recognize her father from Sobibór? My fears were completely unfounded. Her parents entered the room and hugged me. Then her father opened an attaché case. "I collect photos of Hagen's former Jewish population. I give lectures in universities about the Jewish community here, and now I'm going to take you over to the synagogue we're restoring."

"Thank you," I told him. "I would be very happy to see the synagogue with you."

And then he told me, "We have a big schedule for you. Tomorrow we have tickets for the opera. Later in the week we will take you to a concert."

I thought to myself: these are Germans? I thought they were all like Wagner and Gomerski. But at this point I began to understand that not all Germans are bad people. True, some of them had aided in the Holocaust. But I could clearly see that many Germans empathized with my suffering. It was not just the red-carpet treatment that they gave me. Their genuine compassion reminded me of the righteous Poles who had saved me and my brother.

It was soon time to attend the trial. This was history being made, and for me it brought the past right into the present. When I entered the courtroom, I immediately spotted Frenzel, sitting there with a smile on his face, dressed in a nice suit and tie as if he were going to work in an office. But this time I was more prepared than I had been years earlier when I had first seen Gomerski and had allowed my anger to get the best of me. Now I was more focused on doing what needed to be done.

Sitting on the witness stand, I concentrated on presenting the facts about events that I had seen with my own eyes, what he, Frenzel, had done—how he had tortured and killed people. That Frenzel had worked at Sobibór was never in question. But trying to save his neck, Frenzel and his lawyer attempted to downplay his role in the killing process, portraying him as a bystander rather than an active participant. This I could not tolerate. So I called out to Frenzel from the witness stand, for everyone to hear: "For what reason did you come to Sobibór? For a vacation? I'm a living witness. I dealt with you every day."

I retold the story of how Frenzel had beaten me with his whip. I also told of how Frenzel led my friend Mordechaj away after catching him with food I had stolen for him and how thereafter Mordechaj was not seen again in the camp. Mordechaj had said he, not I, was the sole guilty party and had saved my life with his heroism that day. Now I was seeing to it that his murderer received justice.

Frenzel's defense lawyer vigorously interrogated me about my statements. During cross-examination he presented a large map of Sobibór. With a long stick the attorney pointed to the map and asked me to identify the locations of various workshops and barracks that I had described in my testimony. After so many years, it was difficult for me to accurately recall these tiny details. And I had never even seen Sobibór's layout depicted on a map before. It was obvious to everyone in the courtroom that the lawyer was trying to trick me into making small mistakes, thus attempting to cast doubt on my memory of the basic facts to which I had testified. I resented this treatment, and I allowed my feelings to be known. I asked the judge, "Who is on trial here? I came here to be a witness." I also angrily insinuated that Frenzel's attorney could be a Nazi himself. The judge then told the attorney to go a little easier on me. During the recess the attorney approached me and said, "Mr. Bialowitz, I am not a Nazi. I can assure you that I have many Jewish friends."

By this time I was so overwhelmed thinking about what I had gone through during the war that I became sick and felt like fainting. A doctor arrived, and they stopped the trial. After examining me, the doctor declared that I would need several days to recuperate. I called my daughter Simone that evening and asked if she could come to Germany to take care of me. The German government paid for her airplane ticket, and she flew in from New York to look after me for the next two weeks until I completed my testimony. Simone, too, was surprised and moved by the warm hospitality of the German people.

Frenzel's trial took nearly three years to conclude. To my inexpressible relief and satisfaction, his appeal was lost. Frenzel's life sentence was reconfirmed on October 4, 1985. But he never returned to prison. After several appeals the Hagen court issued a final ruling in 1990 stating: "Because the defendant is now seventy-eight years of age and—as determined by this court—now in such a desolate state that, in the court's judgment, enforcing the prison sentence would no longer serve the intentions of the law. A further term in prison would in itself be a threat to the defendant's life."[13] Thus Frenzel was allowed to live his final years in freedom at a retirement home near Hannover, Germany. He died in 1996. As with Gomerski, in Frenzel's old age he received the mercy that he had never showed to any of Sobibór's victims, young or old.

Sometimes people ask whether I can forgive the perpetrators of the Holocaust. I know that forgiveness can be healthy. It has the power to cure me of the hatred toward the murderers that I have carried with me as a burden for more than sixty years. I can surely forgive the perpetrators who tried to help the victims in some way, who tried to be a little more lenient than the rest. But I cannot forgive the sadistic ones, the ones who set out every day to kill as if it were a sport. It is difficult enough to forgive a person who murdered a single human being. But someone who slaughtered thousands of people, including small children? These murderers must pay the price for what they did.

On the other hand, my experience at Frenzel's trial led me to understand that retribution must be reserved only for those who during their lives committed these barbarous acts. Only the murderers should be condemned and punished, not their children and grandchildren. During the trial the courtroom was filled one day with college students there to observe. After my testimony concluded, many of the students came over to hug me and say, "Mr. Bialowitz, this is not our fault. This is our grandparents who did these terrible things. Now we want better relations with the Jewish people." I immediately sympathized with these young people. I asked them to please learn from my testimony about what happened and to tell their children about it so that these things can never happen again. New generations of Europeans should not be made to suffer for wrongdoings with which they had nothing to do. But neither should they ignore their continent's tragic past. They have a responsibility, just as we all do, to study and remember European history so that its worst moments are never repeated in Europe or anywhere else in the world.

Becoming a Public Witness

In 1987 a made-for-television docudrama titled *Escape from Sobibór* aired on the CBS television network. Based on the book by Richard Rashke, it was viewed by millions of people and earned several Golden Globe Awards for its highly effective portrayal of daily life in Sobibór and the revolt that took place there. I was immensely satisfied to know that some of the most important events that took place at Sobibór were captured in a film that so many people watched and would continue to watch for many years into the future. Nevertheless, I regretted that the film could only depict a fraction of the horror and the heroism that occurred at Sobibór. After so many years of not discussing my wartime experiences with my friends and family, I resolved that it was time to help tell the world the story of what happened at Sobibór, just as Sasha and Leon had implored us to do in the moments before we escaped. I would give testimony so that nothing would be forgotten.

I gave my first speech about Sobibór at a Holocaust Remembrance Day event at our local synagogue, Temple Torah, in Little Neck, New York. These programs took place annually and usually included the eyewitness account of a Holocaust survivor. It was difficult for me to share the horrible experiences that I had kept bottled up inside me since the Holocaust. But as soon as I started my presentation, I saw that the entire audience, including the children, listened with rapt attention. I felt a warm connection with the congregation, many of whom were my close friends, and that helped me get through that first presentation. In the end I felt the satisfaction of knowing I had fulfilled an important responsibility. Little did I know it would be the beginning of a new, very meaningful phase in my life: talking to adults and children about the suffering and triumph that I experienced during the Holocaust. Over the past twenty years, I have spoken to groups of adults and children throughout North America, Poland, Germany, and Israel. I have told my stories at schools, universities, synagogues, churches, and museums, and at historical places such as Sobibór and the former Warsaw Ghetto. I have made sure that my videotaped testimony has been recorded for perpetuity by Steven Spielberg's Shoah Foundation, the Yale Holocaust Archive, the United States Holocaust Memorial Museum, the New York Museum of Jewish Heritage, and Israel's official memorial to the victims of the Holocaust, Yad Vashem.

To be sure, my painful memories of the Holocaust will always be with me. I carry a scar on my finger that was sliced by the barbed wire during my escape from Sobibór. I have suffered from insomnia since the Holocaust and have often been awakened by nightmares. One recurring nightmare is of the time I was forced to remove the decomposed bodies from the cattle cars at Sobibór. These memories are not forgettable. But when I tell my story, there is a sure sense of who I am and what I and others did to undermine the machinery of the murderers. In a time of darkness, we resisted and we prevailed.

In 1989 I was invited to appear on a television program titled *The Hunt for Stolen War Treasures*, hosted by Michael York. The producers of the show wished to expose the many thefts that the Nazis had perpetrated. My anticipated role in the production would be to travel to Sobibór with a camera crew. There we would search for the jar of buried valuables that I had left behind in 1943. If found, it would serve as evidence of what the Nazis took from their victims. I received the producer's invitation, however, at a time when Evelyn had just been told by her doctors that she had only six months to live. I told my daughter that I had decided to spend time with her instead of appearing on this television program. But Evelyn said, "No, Daddy, you must go. This is very important." So the producers brought me to both Sobibór and Izbica to search for the valuable items I had hidden underground. If we were to find anything, we planned to donate the proceeds to causes that support destitute and ill survivors of the Holocaust.

It was my first return to Sobibór since 1943. Much had changed. With the exception of a building that now housed a small museum, nearly every structure that I recalled had disappeared when the Germans dismantled the camp after the revolt, in an effort to enforce secrecy about both their crimes and the humiliating defeat that they suffered there. The train tracks remained, as did a rickety, wooden forestry tower that was once the main watchtower in the center of the camp. But otherwise the outline and layout of the camp were barely recognizable anymore. Adding to our difficulty was the fact that the terrain itself had altered dramatically since 1943. Over the decades many new trees had taken root, and it was very difficult to remember exactly where I had hidden the jar. Nevertheless, we dug several holes in areas where I guessed I had buried the jar of valuables. But when I noticed several small, existing holes among the trees, I realized that local residents had probably succeeded long ago in recovering the valuables. We called off the search without finding any trace of the buried jar.

In Izbica we discovered that even the Jewish cemetery had been desecrated in the search for valuables. Open pits dotted the ground where graves once were. Human bones were strewn in various parts of the cemetery. Most of the remaining gravestones, some of which were pockmarked with bullet holes, had toppled. The ground was covered in leaves and bushes. An elderly man who had walked up to the cemetery told me that during the war he had witnessed the shooting of my mother in this place. Though it had been more than forty years since her death, I never knew the exact details. It was painfully emotional news, and I was crying. In my grief I reached down and picked up a skull that I knew could have belonged to my own mother. I could not allow my mother's bones to remain in this cemetery, exposed to both the elements and grave robbers. I therefore decided to bring several of the bones back to New York to be interred in a section of the Jewish cemetery where many former residents of Izbica were buried.

My return flight from Poland included a stopover in Frankfurt, Germany. At the airport a young German security guard at the X-ray machine noticed something suspicious in my carry-on bag. When he opened the bag, he found the bones that I had packed. I could see the shock on his face. He probably wondered if he had caught a murderer. He told me to wait where I was because he needed to call the police. With tears in my eyes, I explained to him that these were the bones of my mother, that she had been shot by a German firing squad during the Holocaust. He responded by saying he could not allow me to take these out of the country, that he could lose his job for doing so. But he was beginning to cry as well. He understood all that this meant to me. He allowed me to take the bones. When I arrived in New York, I contacted the surviving members of Izbica's Jewish community in New York. Many of them joined me at the cemetery for an emotional event. More than four decades after our relatives were murdered and buried in mass graves, together we buried their bones properly, in a ceremony conducted according to the Jewish tradition.

Though it is difficult for many survivors to return to the places where they suffered, I have been able to do so, and it has proven to be a very rewarding part of my life. Since 1987 I have returned to Poland on over a dozen occasions. My visits have allowed me to witness a remarkable rebirth of Jewish life in Poland. In a country where twenty years ago it was nearly impossible for me to find a group of Jews with whom to pray, today thousands of Polish Jews are now embracing their heritage and building a thriving spiritual community, especially in Warsaw. This transformation would never have been possible without the tireless leadership of the talented chief rabbi of Poland, Michael Schudrich, as well as the generous support of two wise and committed philanthropists, Ronald Lauder and Tad Taube. Furthermore, thanks in large part to the support of the City of Warsaw and Poland's Ministry of Culture, the state-of-the-art Museum of the History of Polish Jews is being developed next to the Warsaw Ghetto Uprising Monument. The Polish, Dutch, Slovak, and Israeli governments are partnering to modernize the memorial pavilion at Sobibór by 2013. And the Jewish cemetery of Izbica is no longer a site of desecration: although the cemetery still needs to be restored to the condition merited by its religious and historical prominence, its grounds are periodically tended by junior high school students from Izbica; signs pointing to the locations of the mass graves have been erected; and a memorial has been placed at the front of the cemetery by the government of Germany and the Foundation for the Preservation of Jewish Heritage in Poland.

The Jewish renaissance in Poland not only testifies to the resilience of the Jewish people; it also exemplifies the turning of a new page in both Poland and many other parts of Europe, where diverse groups of people are living together in greater harmony than at past points in history. To be sure, dangerous anti-Semitism and other forms of racism persist through-out Europe and the world. But in my travels many people have expressed a general openness to others and a heartfelt desire to learn about the past through my own life story. Often I have noticed that people are visibly moved by their encounters with me. Their responses have taught me that— as important as books, films, and museums are for teaching the world about genocide—there is no substitute for the powerful impact of meeting a living witness. I am also grateful that some of the people with whom I have spoken have even become my close friends. I have learned as much from them as I hope they have learned from me.

I have also come to believe that, particularly in Poland, the late Pope John Paul II—who enjoyed friendships with Jewish schoolmates in Poland before the Holocaust—deserves immense credit for helping to increase dialogue between Catholics and Jews. During his meaningful visit to the synagogue in Rome in 1986—the first ever such gesture by any pope— Pope John Paul II referred to Jews as "the beloved elder brothers of the Church." These profound words represented the pope's powerful vision that for Christians and Jews to be a blessing to the world, "we must first of all be a blessing to one another."[14] Pope John Paul II advanced this doctrine of "mutual esteem" even further by becoming the first papal leader to establish official bilateral relations with the State of Israel. During his historic visit to the Holy Land in 2000, Pope John Paul II placed a note in the Wailing Wall in Jerusalem asking for God's forgiveness for "the behavior of those who in the course of history have caused these children of yours to suffer." He then contributed all the more to reconciliation by saying: "I assure the Jewish people . . . the Catholic Church is deeply saddened by the hatred, acts of persecution and displays of anti-Semitism directed against the Jews by Christians at any time and in any place."[15] The only pity is that Pope John Paul II was not in command of the Vatican during World War II. If he had held the papacy during those years, I am certain that he would have ordered all Catholics to protect Jews in any way possible. To be sure, many clergy and laypeople risked their lives to aid or rescue Jews during the Holocaust.[16] However, thousands more Jews might have survived had there been a pope who explicitly directed his followers to save the lives of their fellow human beings.

During my visits to Poland, I have been blessed with the opportunity to personally express my deep gratitude to Maria Mazurek and her children. I will always view the entire Mazurek family as angels sent by God. Several of my children have also been fortunate enough to meet and thank the Mazureks for their heroism. During one of our visits to the Mazurek family, Mr. and Mrs. Mazurek's son, Jan, asked me, "If we had been the ones in need, would you have saved us like we saved you?" I answered that I could only hope that I would have been as heroic as his family was. For their incredible deeds, I have officially honored Maria and Michał Mazurek as Righteous among the Nations at Yad Vashem. This award is given to non-Jews who extended a helping hand to save the lives of Jews. It is the highest honor that the Jewish people, through the State of Israel, bestow upon non-Jews. The more than twenty-two thousand role models who have thus far been honored as Righteous among the Nations represent the highest ideals to which human beings can aspire. They are shining lights who prove that it is always possible to resist evil, even under the most challenging circumstances and even as a lone individual. As Elie Wiesel points out: "Let us not forget, after all, that there is always a moment when the moral choice is made. Often because of one story or one book or one person, we are able to make a different choice, a choice for humanity, for life. And so we must know these good people who helped Jews during the Holocaust. We must learn from them, and in gratitude and hope, we must remember them."[17]

Judaism in My Life

My personal experience of Sobibór and the entire Holocaust has kept me closer to my religion than a humdrum existence might have. As a boy I was part of a religiously observant family, but as a teen I became less observant due to the difficulty of carrying out many of the rituals during wartime. By the time I was taken to Sobibór at the age of seventeen, I was still young yet old enough to begin wrestling with my beliefs, something that is encouraged in the Jewish tradition.

The attempted extermination of the Jews and our own brushes with death changed so many of us who wanted to practice our religion as we chose. For some survivors it became impossible to believe in a God who could allow the horror of places such as Auschwitz, Treblinka, Bełżec, Sobibór, and the many killing fields of Eastern Europe. And yet I have chosen to believe in God just as Job did after he endured seemingly endless suffering. God never guarantees justice, though he commands us to pursue it. The Holocaust happened because God allows human beings to allow Holocausts. We are all born with the freedom to constantly choose between good and evil, life and death. People have too often failed to use this freedom appropriately. As my daughter Evelyn's role model, the Reverend Dr. Martin Luther King Jr., once wrote, "More and more I feel that the people of ill will have used time much more effectively than have the people of good will."[18]

To this day I remain part of the Judaism into which I was born. I am an active member of my synagogue who attends services every week on the Sabbath. I thank God for giving me the strength to continue talking regularly about the Holocaust to groups of people around the world. Just as I promised to do on the day of the Sobibór revolt in 1943, I am still bearing witness to what happened at Sobibór and helping the world to remember.

Always Remember

My personal survival and the wonderful family that came from it mean very little if Hitler's legacy of genocide lives on. At Sobibór we fought for a world without prejudice, racism, and genocide. Looking at the world today, we can see that our fight is still not fully successful. I helped to destroy the Sobibór of the Germans, but others have built new Sobibórs. The systematic murder of entire peoples continues into the twenty-first century—just think of the ongoing genocide and mass atrocities in Darfur with hundreds of thousands of civilians slain because of their ethnicity. It is not over.

We must always be aware that unimaginable evil can arise at any time. The leaders of Iran, for example, directly and publicly incite genocide against Jews while developing the nuclear capability they could use to carry out this crime themselves one day. In such dangerous times, vigilant condemnation is necessary but normally not sufficient. We must use all available peaceful means—including, for example, prosecution under international laws that prohibit incitement to commit genocide—to prevent genocide before it occurs. And if prevention fails, we must resist the Hitlers of our generation, not just make speeches and hope someone else is listening. Had the Allied forces simply bombed the railroad tracks that brought millions of victims to the gas chambers, they could have saved many of these people. I and other prisoners of these camps prayed that the passing warplanes would drop bombs directly on top of us. We felt that even if we were killed, our deaths would not have been in vain because at least the gas chambers would have been destroyed. While I am grateful to everyone who fought against the Axis powers to eventually free us, I will always wonder why the world's democracies and their leaders did not do even more to save us. These leaders were confronted with ample evidence of how the Germans murderously destroyed the Warsaw Ghetto and secretly operated death camps. A brave spy, Jan Karski, was sent to these areas by the Polish resistance movement and went on to personally present his eyewitness testimony to the British and American governments in 1942 and again in 1943. In response to Karski's firsthand accounts of German atrocities, however, the Allied leaders changed none of their tactics. Because of this I and my fellow survivors will always feel that we were abandoned by the world in our time of need.

I know that a similar feeling of abandonment is felt by victims of other genocides: Native Americans, Armenians, the Chinese, Cambodians, Bosnians, Rwandans, and most recently the Darfuris. Like me, the few victims of genocide who survive usually do so because they manage to save themselves or are helped by heroic individuals or small groups of people whose consciences lead them to risk their lives to save others. It is a shame that even to this day the world's leaders cannot be depended upon to protect the innocent. This will hopefully change soon. But for now our fates and the fates of our neighbors continue to rest in our very own hands.

I will always mourn the many innocents who perished at Sobibór and throughout the world during World War II. But I will also never forget the brave fighters of Sobibór and heroes like the Catholic farmers who rescued me and my brother from death. They must always be remembered as shining examples of the ability we each have to respond to humankind's worst actions with both physical and spiritual resistance.

We must remember not to forget.

Notes

Introduction

1. Carol Rittner and Sondra Myers, eds., *The Courage to Care: Rescuers of Jews during the Holocaust* (New York: New York University Press, 1986), 124.

2. Ryszard Walczak et al., *Those Who Helped: Polish Rescuers of Jews during the Holocaust, Part 3* (Warsaw: The Main Commission for the Investigation of Crimes against the Polish Nation—The Institute of National Memory, The Polish Society for the Righteous among the Nations, 1997), quoted in Anna Poray, *Polish Righteous: Those Who Risked Their Lives*, 2004, http://www.savingjews.org (accessed January 24, 2010).

Chapter 1. Before War

1. *Kasher* is Hebrew for "fit," used to describe foods fit for consumption by Jews according to traditional Jewish law.

2. *Heder* is Hebrew for "room." A heder was a type of school for Jewish children in Europe where they could receive elementary or slightly more-advanced education in Jewish religion and traditions.

3. "Poaley Syjon" is a Hebrew phrase meaning "Workers of Zion"; it was a movement of non-Marxist Jews committed to social democracy and Jewish nationalism.

4. *Kibbutz* is Hebrew for a collective farm or settlement founded by Jews in Palestine over the years since 1909. *Hachsharah* is Hebrew for "preparation." Hachsharah groups provided intellectual and physical training for *chaluzim*, or "pioneers," intending to settle in Palestine. The groups' main activities involved preparing for life in Palestine by studying Modern Hebrew and working on Polish farms.

5. In Yiddish: "Vos a symcha, vi aangename es iz bay a goy tsu hakn holts."

6. Zeev Jabotinsky founded the New Zionist Organization, also known as the Revisionist Zionist Organization. It was a right-wing and radical faction of the more centrist General Zionist Organization, which existed during the years between the world wars in Poland and other parts of Eastern and Central Europe. Jabotinsky's organization had many

followers in Poland, especially among Jewish youth. See Philip Bialowitz and Joseph Bialowitz, *Bunt w Sobiborze* (Warsaw: Wydawnictwo Nasza Księgarnia, 2008), 30–31.

7. *Challah* is the Hebrew term for the braided style of bread found throughout Central Europe and the Slavic countries and traditionally eaten by Jews on the Sabbath and during festivals.

8. The literal meaning of the Hebrew word *tzedaka* is "justice"; it also signifies the Jewish custom requiring that people help their less fortunate neighbors in any way possible.

9. *Gut shabbes* is Yiddish for "Have a good Sabbath."

10. *Kindel* is Yiddish for "little child."

11. "Fiszele" is a diminutive form of the name "Fiszel" in Yiddish.

12. *Matze* is the Yiddish word for "unleavened bread"; it is eaten by Jews during the annual Passover holiday to commemorate their ancestors' hasty exodus from slavery in Egypt. This ritually prescribed bread is one of the chief symbols of the Passover holiday.

13. *Kashrus* is the Hebrew word referring to the Jewish dietary laws.

14. *Chollent* is a Yiddish word for a hearty stew comprised of beef, beans, and potatoes.

15. *Tzitzis* is the Hebrew term for the four spun woolen fringes attached to a four-cornered garment that observant Jews wear every day to remind them of the 613 commandments listed in the Torah. Blue tzitzis were prescribed in the book of Numbers when God instructed Moses: "Speak to the Israelite people and instruct them to make for themselves fringes on the corners of their garments throughout the ages; let them attach a cord of *tekhelet* [Hebrew for "blue"] to the fringe at each corner. That shall be your fringe; and when you see it, you will remember all the commandments of God and perform them." According to the Talmud, the blue color was mandated because "*tekhelet* resembles the sea and the sea resembles the sky and the sky resembles God's holy throne" (*Menachot* 43b). The dye was supposed to come from an animal called the "hillazon," but sometime after the Jews were exiled from the Land of Israel, the manufacturing of this dye became increasingly rare until finally no one remembered what this mysterious animal was, and the use of blue tzitzis was therefore abandoned. Then in the mid-nineteenth century, Rabbi Gershon Henoch Leiner of Radzyń, who was the grandson of Izbica's famous Rabbi Mordechaj Joseph Leiner, fantastically claimed to have rediscovered the secret of producing the beautiful dye. However, most tzitzis-wearing Polish Jews beyond Radzyń and Izbica continued to wear white tzitzis.

16. These are all Yiddish terms: *flanken* is a specific cut of beef, *simmis* is mashed sweet potatoes, *kugel* is a sweet noodle casserole, and *ruggelach* is a type of sweet pastry.

17. *Kristallnacht* is the German term referring to "The Night of Broken Glass," during which Jewish businesses were vandalized throughout Germany, hundreds of Jews were attacked, and thousands of Jewish men were rounded up and taken to concentration camps.

18. *Juden* is German for "Jews."

19. Rabbi Mordechaj Joseph Leiner founded the Hasidic dynasty known as the Izbica Radzyń dynasty. His grave can be found at the Jewish cemetery in Izbica. The Izbica

Radzyń dynasty currently thrives in the town of Bnei Brak in the State of Israel (Bialowitz, *Bunt w Sobiborze*, 41). The teaching cited here diverges from Rabbi Hanina's maxim: "All is in the hands of Heaven except for reverence for Heaven."

20. "Im ba l'hargekha, hashkem l'hargo" (*Berachot* 58a and 62b; *Yoma* 85b; *Sanhedrin* 72a).

21. *Chazzan* is Hebrew for "cantor," the musician trained in the vocal arts who leads a synagogue congregation in prayer.

22. *Bimah* is the Hebrew word describing a synagogue's elevated area or platform intended to serve as the standing place for the person either reading the Torah or leading the congregation in prayer.

Chapter 2. War Begins

1. *Payes* is Hebrew for "corners," "sides," or "edges"; they are the side curls worn by religious Jewish men in observance of the commandment in Leviticus 19:27: "You shall not round off the edge-growth of your head nor ruin the edge of your beard."

2. "Majn Jidysze Mame" is Yiddish for "My Jewish Mother."

3. The Prayer for Travelers: "May it be your will, Lord our God and God of our fathers, to lead us in peace and direct our steps in peace; to guide us in peace, to support us in peace, and to bring us to our destination in life, joy and peace. Deliver us from the hands of every enemy and lurking foe, from robbers and wild beasts on the journey, and from all kinds of calamities that may come to and afflict the world; and bestow blessing upon all our actions. Grant me grace, kindness, and mercy in your eyes and in the eyes of all who behold us and bestow bountiful kindness upon us. Hear the voice of our prayer, for you hear everyone's prayer. Blessed are you, Lord, who hears prayer."

4. The regular German Armed Forces occupied all Polish territories from September until the end of October 1939. On October 26, 1939, a German civil government and police force composed of Gestapo, gendarmerie, and police divisions assumed overall governance of a part of occupied Poland renamed by the Germans as the "General Government." Izbica fell within the boundaries of the General Government (Bialowitz, *Bunt w Sobiborze*, 53).

5. *Tompehoizen* is a Yiddish word referring to a particular style of knee-length shorts.

6. The Germans mandated the wearing of a Star of David armband by all Jews in the General Government beginning in October 1939. Jews wore the Star of David on their chests in other occupied countries. The Jews of Germany were forced to wear Stars of David beginning in 1941 (Bialowitz, *Bunt w Sobiborze*, 58).

7. *Judenrat* is German for "Jewish Council." The Judenrat was a coalition of local Jewish elders appointed by the Germans to serve as liaisons between the Jews and the Germans. The Judenrat was complicit, occasionally well intentioned, but often serving only its members, who were regarded with deep ambivalence by the Jewish community. But since these

men had the power to send to or keep people from the work details and the camps, Jews often strove to attain their favor. It was tacitly known that the Judenrat officials were not above bribery. Those with the prescience and the means to avoid the work details and the camps gave what they could to be spared from the Judenrat's lists.

8. *Volksdeutscher* is a German term meaning "member of the German people." The term was popularized by the Nazis to designate people who spoke German as their mother tongue, but who lived outside the Reich and were citizens of another country.

9. *Akcja* is Polish for "action," used to refer to a roundup by authorities.

10. *Bejt Jaakow* is a Hebrew term referring to a small school in which girls can study Jewish subjects.

11. Many of these people arrested in Izbica were sent to a Gestapo-run prison at the castle in Lublin. From there they were transported to Auschwitz or to concentrations camps in Germany (Bialowitz, *Bunt w Sobiborze*, 62).

12. *Halachah* is Hebrew for "Jewish Law" or "the path."

13. *Shochet* is the Hebrew word referring to a slaughterer who follows the laws of kashrus.

14. *Schlepp* is Yiddish for "transport."

15. The Gestapo was the official secret police of Nazi Germany. It operated under the overall authority of the SS (the Schutzstaffel, or "Shield Squadron") and was legislatively exempted from any judicial oversight. The roughly forty-five thousand members of the Gestapo were responsible for countless wartime atrocities, ranging from individual attacks on civilians to overall administration of the concentration camps.

16. *Unterscharführer* was the German military rank equivalent of corporal; *Rottenführer* was the equivalent of private first class.

17. After the German aggression against the Soviet Union in 1941, Germans actively recruited Soviet prisoners of war to aid the German forces in a variety of capacities, including forced removal of Jews from the ghettos and guard duty at concentration and extermination camps. Referred to by Polish Jews as "Ukrainians," these volunteers in fact came from all over the Soviet Union, though mostly from Ukraine, Estonia, Latvia, and Lithuania. Some "Ukrainians" may have chosen to enlist in the German cause because the alternative was starvation in a prisoner of war camp; however, after enlisting they often surpassed Germans in their cruelty toward Jews. The Germans used a special training camp (called an SS-Ausbildungslager) in Trawniki, near Izbica, to train these turncoats. The Germans referred to them as *Hiwis* (ancillary division). For a fuller explanation of the "Ukrainian" subject, see Jules Schelvis, *Sobibór: A History of a Nazi Death Camp* (New York: Berg, 2007), 34–36.

18. *Shivah* is the Hebrew word referring to the ritually prescribed period of mourning observed by Jews, usually lasting one week.

19. Between March and May 1942, ten thousand Jews were deported to Izbica from Germany and Nazi-occupied Czechoslovakia. The Germans promised these Jews that they were being resettled in "the East" for work assignments. In fact, there were no jobs for them

in Izbica. The town was only a "transfer ghetto" where the Germans planned to keep these Jews in primitive conditions for a period of weeks or months prior to sending them to the death camps located in the Lubelski District. Many of these deportees died of hunger and illness in Izbica (Bialowitz, *Bunt w Sobiborze*, 76).

Chapter 3. The Rosenbergers

1. The Yiddish language originated as a variety of Middle High German.

2. *Bar mitzvah* is the Hebrew term referring to the ceremony marking the point at which a Jewish male becomes accountable for following the commandments contained in Jewish Law.

3. *Seder* is Hebrew for "order," used to refer to the ceremonious annual dinners in which Jews retell the story of their ancestors' exodus from Egypt.

Chapter 4. Fritz

1. *Malach hamavet* is Hebrew for "angel of death."

2. The *She'ma* is a Hebrew prayer central to the Jewish religion. It is recited daily and, if possible, in the moments before one's death.

3. Official German records show that both Herta and Ilse Rosenberger were on a list of children eligible for immigration to Great Britain but that ultimately they did not avail themselves of their spots. For more information, see Konstanze Ertel, "Herta Rosenberger," *Gedenkbuch für die Karlsruher Juden* [Memorial Book for the Karlsruhe Jews], February 2005, http://my.informedia.de/gedenkbuch.php?PID=12&name=3565&seite=2&suche=R (accessed January 24, 2010). This opportunity was available to Herta and Ilse via the Kindertransport (German for "child transport"), which is the informal name for a multifaith effort that attempted to rescue Jewish children prior to the outbreak of World War II. The rescue operation was first proposed in the United Kingdom just a few days after the events of Kristallnacht in November 1938 and was approved by the British government soon thereafter. Beginning in December 1938, approximately nine thousand to ten thousand children, some seventy-five hundred of them Jewish, were brought from Germany, Austria, Czechoslovakia, and Poland to Great Britain. The last transport to Great Britain left from the Netherlands on May 14, 1940. For more information, see United States Holocaust Memorial Museum, *Kindertransport, 1938–1940*, 2009, http://www.ushmm.org/wlc/article.php?ModuleId=10005260 (accessed January 24, 2010).

Chapter 5. Summer 1942

1. "Rachem Na" is Hebrew for "Please Have Pity."

2. *Mensch* is Yiddish for "ethical person."

Chapter 6. Fall 1942

1. *Meshuggah* is Yiddish for "crazy."

Chapter 7. November 1942 to April 1943

1. *Judenrein* is German for "cleansed of Jews."

2. In the weeks between mid-October and early November 1942, the Germans attempted to murder all of Izbica's Jews. Approximately one thousand Jews were transported to the death camps of Bełżec and Sobibór. If the Germans could not find available train space for Jews, they amassed the Jews at the movie house before marching them to the Jewish cemetery of Izbica. During the first several days of November 1942, approximately one thousand Jews were shot in the cemetery and buried in mass graves (Bialowitz, *Bunt w Sobiborze*, 115).

3. Between 1935 and 1945, the German armed forces were called the Wehrmacht.

4. *Judenstadt* is German for "Jewish city."

5. Throughout the General Government, the Germans developed "residual ghettos" to entice any remaining Jews to come out of hiding. Jews who could not survive the harsh conditions of the forest had little choice but to return to these ghettos. By the middle of 1943, all these ghettos were closed and their citizens were transported to death camps (Bialowitz, *Bunt w Sobiborze*, 123).

6. *Kaddish* is the Jewish prayer of mourning, traditionally recited by a mourner after the death of a parent, spouse, sibling, or child.

7. The zloty is the currency of Poland.

8. *Minyan* is the Hebrew word referring to prayer groups of at least ten persons.

9. *Sonderkommando* was a German term meaning "special unit," which the Nazis used to describe work units of death-camp prisoners forced to aid the killing process.

Chapter 8. Life in Sobibór

1. Everyone in Sobibór referred to the three camps in German: Lager 1, Lager 2, and Lager 3.

2. *Schwarzbrot* is German for "dark rye bread."

3. *Bahnhofkommando* is German for "station brigade."

4. "Lustiger Floh" is German for "Merry Flea," "Gottes Heimat" for "God's Own Home," and "Schwalbennest" for "Swallow's Nest."

5. *Himmelstrasse* is German for "road to heaven."

6. *Oberscharführer* is the German military rank equivalent to a staff sergeant.

7. In 1942 hair collected from humans in every concentration camp was utilized to produce industrial filters, woven into yarn, and used to make slippers for U-boat crews and stockings for staff of the Reichsbahn (the German national rail company). See Schelvis, *Sobibór*, 72.

8. "Ratuj moje dziecko!" ("Save my baby!" in Polish).

9. A possible cause of these passengers' deaths may be found in the eyewitness account of Jan Karski, who provided this description of how Jews were loaded into cattle cars in Izbica: "Before the Jews got in, a layer of quicklime was emptied onto the floors of the carriages. Officially, it was to serve as a hygienic measure preventing the spread of infectious diseases. In reality, the lime very quickly absorbed the humidity of the air, causing an increase in the oxygen so that people began to suffocate. At the same time, lime that came into contact with human excrement exuded toxic substances such as chlorine that led to suffocation. The Nazis achieved a double goal. Diseases were not transmitted and it was easier to wash down the railroad cars once the people got off. Also, a number of Jews died during the journey, which was what the Nazis actually hoped for." For more information, see Jan Karski, *Tajne państwo: Opowieść o polskim podziemiu* [Secret State: The Story of the Polish Underground] (Warsaw: Twój Styl, 1999), quoted in Yarek Shalom, *Virtual Shtetl: Izbica*, 2009, 4, http://www.sztetl.org.pl/en/article/izbica/5,history/ (accessed January 24, 2010).

10. *Waldkommando* is German for "forest brigade."

11. "We are just good guys / that want to kno-o-w. / That's why we go, that's why we go. / We are just good guys / that want to kno-o-w. / That's why we go—everywhere! / (Refrain) / Everywhere! Everywhere! / Where the girls are, where the girls are. / Everywhere! Everywhere! / Where the girls are there is the ball!"

12. The Dutch word *tof* (meaning "good") contained in the lyrics of "Overal, Overal!" is an example of a Yiddish word (*tof* or *tov*) that entered the Dutch language at some point during the centuries-long history of Jewish life in the Netherlands. One could speculate that the Dutch Jewish prisoners chose to sing this melody because they enjoyed its Yiddish-influenced lyrics and/or they thought that Sobibór's many Yiddish-speaking prisoners would appreciate the song all the more.

Chapter 9. Planning Vengeance

1. "Nekome, nekome" (Yiddish for "Vengeance, vengeance").

2. "Nemmt nekome!" (Yiddish for "Take vengeance!").

Chapter 10. Escape from Sobibór

1. Sukkot is the Hebrew term for "the Feast of Tabernacles."

2. Based on the verse found in Leviticus 18:5, "And you shall keep my statutes and my judgments, which if a man does, he shall live by them," the rabbis of the Talmudic period concluded that lifesaving supersedes even the commandments to observe the Sabbath and the Day of Atonement (*Sanhedrin* 85 and 74a).

3. Only after the end of the war did the consequences of the revolt at Sobibór become more fully known. As many as twelve SS men and two Ukrainian guards were killed during

the revolt. Immediately following the revolt, Reichsführer-SS (General of the Army) Heinrich Himmler ordered that the entire camp be destroyed and planted over with trees. About 275 Jews were brought from Treblinka to accomplish this task before they were killed in November 1943 (Schelvis, *Sobibór*, 189). According to one of the most detailed analyses of available information, of the roughly 650 Jews at the camp on October 14, 1943, about 365 tried to escape during the revolt. All of the estimated 285 Jews who did not attempt escape were killed in the days following the revolt. Of the estimated 365 who attempted escape, 158 were killed during the revolt by bullets or mines. By October 23, 1943, the Germans had recaptured and killed an additional 107 of the escapees. At least 23 escapees were murdered by non-Germans before the war ended. Some prisoners are likely to have escaped but may have died of illness while in hiding, thus leaving their ultimate fates unknown. Only 47 prisoners of Sobibór, including five men who escaped from the Waldkommando prior to the revolt, are known to have survived until the end of the war (Schelvis, *Sobibór*, 182). After the Sobibór uprising, Himmler also ordered the killing of all Jewish prisoners in the Lubelski district. The stated reason was that these Jews had become a threat to the Third Reich, but this was probably a pretext for the crime to follow. During "Aktion Erntefest," which was carried out between November 3 and 4, 1943, the Germans murdered 42,000 Jews from the Lubelski district, including nearly every Jewish prisoner held at the camps at Majdanek, Trawniki, and Poniatowa (Bialowitz, *Bunt w Sobiborze*, 209).

Chapter 11. New Dangers

1. Armia Krajowa is Polish for the "Home Army." The AK was the dominant resistance movement in German-occupied Poland and was active in all areas of the country from September 1939 until its disbanding in January 1945.

2. It is probable that these cattle cars were carrying not Jews but rather Polish peasants from the Zamojski region who were dispossessed by the Germans and transported to the Majdanek concentration camp during the summer of 1944 (Bialowitz, *Bunt w Sobiborze*, 218).

Chapter 12. Liberation and Victory

1. The Perec House was named after the famous Yiddish writer from Zamość, Icchak Lejbusz Perec.

2. To this day, Leon Feldhendler's murder remains unsolved (Bialowitz, *Bunt w Sobiborze*, 235).

3. "L'chaim" is Hebrew for "To life!"

Chapter 13. Life as a Displaced Person

1. Prior to the war, Jews accounted for about 90 percent of Izbica's population of five thousand and 10 percent of Poland's population of thirty-three million. Of the estimated

six million Polish citizens who died as a result of the war, up to three million of these were Polish Jews. Given a prewar population of about 3.3 million Jews in Poland, this means that only one of every ten Polish Jews survived the war. For a full explanation of these statistics, see Israel Gutman and Robert Rozett, "Estimated Jewish Losses in the Holocaust," in *Encyclopedia of the Holocaust*, ed. Israel Gutman (New York: Macmillan, 1990), 4:1799. See also Raul Hilberg, *The Destruction of the European Jews*, 3rd ed. (New Haven, CT: Yale University Press, 2003), 3:1321.

2. "Irgun" or "Irgun Zva'i Le'umi" is a Hebrew phrase meaning "National Military Organization"; it was an armed Jewish underground organization that operated from 1931 until the State of Israel was established in 1948.

Epilogue: Life after Sobibór

1. Bialowitz, *Bunt w Sobiborze*, 56.

2. Schelvis, *Sobibór*, 247.

3. Thomas Blatt, *Sobibór: The Forgotten Revolt* (Issaquah, WA: HEP, 1995), 114. According to Blatt, after the revolt Pechersky made his way back to the Soviet Union and rejoined the Red Army. He was wounded and received a medal for bravery. However, the Soviet authorities subsequently convicted him of treason because he had surrendered to the Germans. The fact that he was wounded when he was taken prisoner was of no matter to the authorities. After a period of time spent in the gulag, he was released because of repeated inquiries about his fate from Holocaust survivors living abroad.

4. Schelvis, *Sobibór*, 255, 247, 258.

5. "We Are Not the Last People of Yesterday: How the Supervisor of the Sobibór Extermination Camp Was Found," *Der Spiegel*, June 12, 1978, 128–33.

6. Alan Levy, *Nazi Hunter: The Wiesenthal File* (New York: Carroll and Graff, 2002), 384.

7. "Brazil Rejects Four Pleas for Accused Nazi's Ouster," *New York Times*, June 22, 1979; "Brazil Is Criticized for Its Refusal to Allow Extradition of Ex-Nazi," *New York Times*, June 24, 1979.

8. Levy, *Nazi Hunter*, 385.

9. "Former Nazi Officer Commits Suicide in Brazil," *New York Times*, October 4, 1980.

10. Blatt, *Sobibór*, 113–14.

11. Schelvis, *Sobibór*, 264.

12. Ibid., 253.

13. Decision by the Landgericht Hagen of January 10, 1990, quoted in Schelvis, *Sobibór*, 254.

14. Rabbi David Rosen, "'Nostra Aetate', Forty Years after Vatican II: Present and Future Perspectives," Conference of the Holy See Commission for Religious Relations with Jewry, Rome, October 27, 2005, http://www.vatican.va/roman_curia/pontifical_councils/chrstuni/relations-jews-docs/rc_pc_chrstuni_doc_20051027_rabbi-rosen_en.html (accessed January 24, 2010).

15. British Broadcasting Corporation, "Pope Prays for Holocaust Forgiveness," *On This Day: 1950–2005,* http://news.bbc.co.uk/onthisday/hi/dates/stories/march/26/newsid _4168000/4168803.stm (accessed January 24, 2010).

16. An extensive compilation of actions by Polish Catholic clergy to assist Jews during the Holocaust can be found in Mark Paul, *Wartime Rescue of Jews by the Polish Catholic Clergy: The Testimony of Survivors,* October 2009, http://www.savingjews.org/docs/clergy _rescue.pdf (accessed January 24, 2010).

17. Rittner and Myers, *Courage to Care,* x.

18. Martin Luther King Jr., *Why We Can't Wait* (New York: Signet Classics, 2000), 74.